THE ROAD WITHIN

The small steps we take to find out who we are

Bob Balinado

3 February 2023

Tracy,

Thank you for being a part of our family.

God bless you always.

Tito Bob

CONTENTS

To Maria.

In gratitude

for the love in your heart

and the work of your hands.

PROLOGUE

"WAITING FOR YOUR BOOK."

My friend Nadette said this to me in one of my rare posts on Facebook. My aunt Wendy also said the same thing. Always inspiring in her words, she's my version of Wendy in JM Barrie's Peter Pan - always a fountain of happy thoughts (incidentally, her husband's name is also Peter).

Carpe diem. My musings always depended on where sanity would lead my fingers on the text box. I always hasten to write my thoughts on my phone notes impromptu wherever and whenever I can, lest my thoughts are lost forever. For the times that I did, I felt I just had to let go, unmindful of formal prose and just allowing my soul to leap onto the pages, all raw but genuine in their moment.

What you read here you probably have learned on your first day at school, and it may be that you were just lost in all the romps and fantasies of childhood. But what you'll find here happens to everyone, and how these would mean to you will make the difference. Life is pretty much the same with all that it offers, but it is the choices we make that will lead us to different paths.

As we carve our own, while we slowly discover all the monotony, we also find that it wears different faces. Like a mute and mysterious harlequin, it awaits us to make the first move and see how we react. Familiar face or not, the road within us determines where we end.

Now that you're holding this book, there must be something deep within you that seeks to fill a void. Our soul is full of non-essential stuff that takes away space that good and happy things should occupy.

As you go through the pages, I can almost see you shrug and say, "Been there, done that!"

Fine. I shall have accomplished my task then.

And why do I say this?

Because it means that I shall have reminded you of the dreams you let go and did not chase; of the doors you did not knock to enter and would have discovered opportunities, of the questions you did not ask because your doubts prevailed; of the steps forward that you did not take, and I shall have reminded you of the truth that you did not seek.

But like all we've learned in life, there is always the need to be reminded and gently led back. As you read through the experiences here, you are also taken into yours. Although this might be an egregious presumption because we are all different and unique, the fact is that it is really a challenge I address to myself. How you react is something I have no control over. You can consign this book to oblivion or keep it on your nightstand. What matters to me is that, somehow, you'll pick a line or two that you can keep in your pocket as you go down the road. When you do that, I hope it will take you to your own path, which no one has trod before. And that's all that I need.

If you were to be given a test about life and how you lived it, treat this book as a reviewer.

On my first day in grade school, we were taught the ABCs. A is for Apple, B for Bell, C for Cat, D for Dog, and E for Elephant. We were taught about relationships in the simplest ways as children do - how David and Ann play with their dog Zip at the park. Today, as adults, we still love to play at the park – but this time with our children and grandchildren. So, in this sense, life is a pleasant continuum.

We would recite the English alphabet repeatedly as my teacher Missus Tan would tap the letters on the board with her pointer stick. It was a memory exercise that could either send you to the Idiot Corner or get you a kiss on your cheek by your mom when you got home.

As grown-ups, we now sit in a bigger classroom we call Life. Your teacher's long dead, the Idiot Corner's banished, and your mom's long gone. This time you're facing your battles alone, and the world keeps its eyes on you and will judge you. Although the game's changed and penalties have become harsher, the simple rules that you followed in Kindergarten will still make you survive and win.

So, let's get back to the basics and get a good grip on it. Go over them like it was our first day in school. When we do that, we'll be surprised to find that life is not at all complicated. It could become as simple as the ABC as we used to know. All we need to do is to embrace it like a long-lost friend - because, after this time, it may be a friend we've just taken for granted.

Life's lessons are not learned best in research papers and theses. They are not learned in the halls of academia or through doctorate diplomas, nor are they found in boardrooms high up in the towers.

We learn wisdom from life's lessons through the joys, pains, trials, and failures we experience every day.

So, let me take you back to my little blue-and-white classroom many years ago.

In the corner is our sandbox, where all the dirty little hands and wooden toys play together.

In the sand, all the wisdom we need to this day still lies.

Life is a cup.

For every love and affection you give -

it fills.

Chapter One

The Story of the Four Cups

I usually get up at five o'clock in the morning, whether I hit the bed late or early the night before. It is a routine I follow simply because I have to prepare breakfast for everyone leaving to work for the day, with Maria at the earliest and the twins later at eight.

This morning as I waited for the coffee to brew, I noticed a neatly packed lunch ready on the table with two candy bars on top. I asked Maria who it was for, as she usually prints the name on post-it notes, but this had none. Quite busy removing the cutleries from the dishwasher without looking up, she said it was for Leandro. I gently rubbed her back and said, "you're such a good mother; you've been doing this since they were small, now they're twenty-five, and you're still doing it."

Her answer was something I did not expect.

She said, "My mother didn't do that to me."

Her reply took me back to when I was a small boy. It was my grandmother who prepared my breakfasts. She'd roll the wooden *batidor* between her palms to stir the hot cocoa made from ground and roasted cacao beans; then she'd pour the hot chocolate into a teapot made of old silver as was the custom. On the other hand, my mother would do the major projects - my birthday cakes and pastries. She had a complete set of cake-decorating paraphernalia made of shiny aluminum, which she took great care of like it was the Crown Jewels. I reckon they must have cost a fortune during her time because she made sure they'd be locked in her glass kitchen cabinet.

My grandmother died when I was ten, so my mom took over, taking care of all my needs, from my breakfasts to my school uniform. When I first attended kindergarten, she would wait for me outside the classroom; and when I moved up to first grade, she was hired to teach the B Section of Grade One. I was in the A section. Since both sections were using the same textbooks introduced by the Irish Jesuits (Here We Come by Sister M. Marguerite), she would tutor me in reading when we got home.

By the time I was in grade three, competition among my classmates had heated up, yet probably fiercer beyond our classrooms where the chaperoning mothers would idly wait and compare notes. I struggled in Arithmetic. Although my mom would tutor me when we got home, I still could not get the numbers right in my thick skull. The smart boys were always called to the front to show their answers on the board. I don't remember ever going to the front, much less solving the numbers. Looking back, I think it did not encourage slow learners to catch up with the smart ones. On the contrary, it might have frozen them in fear, thinking they'd be next on the board: some kids, especially those seated at the front, actually peed in their pants.

And this learning style carried forward to the higher years, unwittingly wedging a vast chasm between the smart ones and those struggling. As more students struggled, the school added more sections after the As and Bs. They now had sections C, D, and E. The farther from A, the older, the bigger and brawnier the kids were, but of course, I don't mean anything here.

In Japan, struggling is part of learning and is not seen as a disability. In the late seventies, a teacher from the University of Michigan went to Japan to study their learning styles. He sat in a fourth-grade class where the students were taught how to draw a three-dimensional cube. He noted that there was a student who struggled to do the cube. The teacher called the struggling student to the front to do the cube on the board. The observer expected the student to break down in tears, but he did not. Instead, he went up to the board and painstakingly struggled to do the cube while everyone patiently waited for him to draw it correctly. When he finally did it right, the class rose in cheers. Elsewhere in the world, students are taught that struggle is a sign of weakness - off from the normal. But in Japan, the students are made to understand that struggle is part of the learning process.

And so, I believe it is with life.

As I've written all over this book, life will always be a mix of triumphs and struggles – in both instances, we always learn, especially if shared with others. Struggling to overcome a weakness is a sure sign of winning. Winning without struggle and preparation will always be empty.

While my mother tried to do her part to make sure I coped and learned, I failed to do my share. I later realized that she could only do so much. Beyond that, everything was out of her control. That's probably why I struggled largely during my grade school years: I did not try hard enough to meet her expectations. I simply didn't care for things that did not interest me – Arithmetic, Health, Science, and Social Studies – I could have yawned out, "who cares?" But there's one thing that's certain: Mothers can see way far into our future beyond what we see. That's why they don't ask us to do things; they 'tell' us to do things.

But I performed well in other things. She'd make me memorize poems she wrote by hand in my notebook. I did the Henry Wadsworth Longfellow poem, The Arrow and the Song which I recited in front of the whole grade school at the gymnasium, and in Grade Two, I did the Charge of the Light Brigade by Lord Alfred Tennyson. Even with the great imbalance of learning, I still did get to march on stage to get a ribbon or two during the Reading of Honors. For a long time, well into my adulthood, I believed that I was a dumbo who deserved to be seated at the back of the classroom until somebody came up with the study that there are four intelligence quotients. But in all those years of struggle, I did whatever class lessons were given to me despite everything - including the strict academic regimen my mother imposed. Indeed, God loves boys who are brave, strong, and true – brave to even try, strong not to break down and cry, and true when they admit their idiocy.

Now, why do I say all these? Looking back now, I feel like I was too regimented - something I wouldn't want my children to be. My mother wanted to fill a void in her that she might not have filled – chances she could have taken but have failed, and somehow, she might have realized that catching her lost opportunities was only through me. She could have wished to stand on a platform and do poetry reading but could have shuddered short as she faced her limitations. Perhaps, making me do those things she failed to do was more fulfilling for herself than for me.

As I went through my teens, perhaps realizing that her magic of tutelage had waned, she just let go - jettisoning me precariously to face the world on my own.

I'd go out at nine in the evening and hang out with older guys at my friend Knicky Pearl's house. We'd drink, smoke, watch 8mm films and imagine we were Crosby, Stills, Nash and Young - and my mom and dad didn't even look for me. I'd come home at about one in the morning after deodorizing my smoky scent with Brut Faberge to make sure, but I'd still hear my dad snore on his bed.

I lived in a small city where everyone seemed to know one another, so I think that worked for my freedom. The only time I remember my folks were still up waiting for me even after midnight was when they found out that I stole the car - and they caught me twice after that. Recidivists get harsher punishments, and so, after that, I'd only go on dates chauffeured by our elderly driver Mauro.

All the person I've become is a product of the choices I made from the time I was in grade school up to this moment. The good days when my cup had run over with all the love and affection my folks gave me *stand equal with* the worst days when I made wrong decisions.

To become precious not only in the eyes of men but, most importantly, God's, there must be an amalgamation of our best and worst in all the coarseness of life. To become God's gold, we must go through life's crucibles of fire - and this daunting task falls on our parent's shoulders.

And as we go through this long-drawn process, our parents pick up the task from the moment we are born and usher us out into this world. As the first goldsmiths of our lives, they put all the good things in our cups, empty from the start - like mercury and ore, metaphorically to mold us into gold.

In the Book of Exodus, there were four cups that the Israelites used in the Passover. It is a Seder rite where they eat bread, drink wine, and pray. Jesus was part of this holy tradition, being born in Bethlehem (meaning "the House of Bread").

The first cup is called the *Sanctification Cup*. It is the "I will take you out of Egypt" cup. The Second is the *Deliverance Cup* or the "I will free you" cup, and the third is the *Redemption Cup* – which is believed to be the cup that Jesus and the apostles used during the Last Supper when He said, "My blood of the covenant which I pour out for the forgiveness of sins." And the last cup is the *Cup of Praise,* where Jesus takes the people as His own.

We are our parent's cups.

From the moment we are born, they begin to pour everything they dream of us to become into our cups. When they brought us to church for baptism, we were the Sanctification Cup - ransomed out from original sin. When we did our Sacrament of Confirmation, we were the Deliverance Cup as we denounced evil; and when we took our first Holy Communion, we were the Redemption Cup as we were finally set free from sin to start on our own. And as we sailed towards the destinies we chose as adults, our parents continued to praise God for what we were to become in His constant grace. This time we became the eternal Praise Cups.

And so, therefore, life is also like a cup.

Let me take you to that day when your parents saw you squint as you faced the light of day for the first time. You were the little cup into which they'd gently pour all their love and affection.

Your cup would fill to the brim for every little deed of care and attention they gave you each day. As you grew old and made your own decisions, your cup began to wear out with holes as they did not remain impervious. For every negative thing you did, you punched a hole in it, and as you jaunted carelessly unmindful of these things, your cup became like sieves in the end – holding nothing, turning your life upside down and empty.

With life's ups and downs, the water levels in your cup will rise and fall with the direction you take. The truly blessed ones die with cups full of everything they have wished for in life, whatever that may be. While some die with cups half-full, some die with empty cups.

But let me say this: Nobody knows whether your cup is full or half full. Some die with their dreams fulfilled, while some die even before their dreams leave the heart and mind. In both instances, though, it is always relative and uniquely personal. Whether the cup is full or half-empty, only the beholder's point of view will matter– everything else will not.

What do I mean by this?

In the circle of life, the things that we could only have wished for as a child but never had, we try to fill into our children's cups. Some of the things we pour into our children's cups are those our parents failed to give us. And the things our parents may have failed to provide us could be what they may not have received as a child. While they were trying to fill our cups, they too, had their own cups to fill - out of the need to make up for those they did not get. This process involves years and years of trying. Some die trying without seeing the circle close.

The people who say they had a happy childhood are those whose cups were filled to the brim by their parents and friends when they were young. Rarely does anyone talk about the price paid for filling those cups. It may have cost the parents a leg and an arm, but that's what parents are for, and some sadly die without being thanked for it.

In this book, I wrote about a friend who never saw his cup reaching full, as he suddenly died while struggling to fill it. But his story is also one of the greatest redemption stories I know. Today, his children enjoy the fruits of his struggles.

Every day Maria and I, for every little chance that we get, try to fill the cups of our children and grandchildren. We've even created our expanded family that includes good friends. Today, we could only wish all these loved ones would drink from the cups we fill and become brave, strong, and true. Inversely, we also drink from our cup as these loved ones and friends fill it - never mind the pinch of poison they sometimes throw, as we have always prayed for the discernment to know what's God's and what's not. Real friends only put the good in each other's cups. Otherwise, like medicines, the bitter syrup will only make one better – even over himself.

So, never let a day pass without pouring all the good things into your child's cup. Every time you say "I love you" to them, you're filling their cup; whenever they'd call you on the phone asking if you're okay, your cup fills. When I call Maria on the phone and bless her, her cup fills; every time we'd call our grandchildren on the phone and do facetime, we'd be filling each other's cups.

My dad passed away abruptly from a massive heart attack. The moment he was gone, my cup was never filled again like it used to, but I take solace in the thought that good memories of him will always fill in - and they're forever because goodness does not die. People die, but their goodness lives on.

For whatever my dad or mom did not complete in my cup, I now make up with my children's cups. That's why I always call them even in the middle of the night if they're not home yet at a particular hour – something that was not done to me in my teen years. I was never asked how my evening was - even when I faced them at the breakfast table the morning after. By doing these now, I am bridging the gap of a circle half-formed.

My parents may have their incomplete circles, but that doesn't stop me from completing mine while I live. And each day, as I fill the cups of my family and friends, the circle comes close to full.

When Maria prepared that packed lunch for Leandro and said, "My mother didn't do that to me," she was completing her own circle -

the circle of life.

Do good.

Speak good.

Be significant -

and that's all.

CHAPTER TWO

ONE GOOD PLUS ONE GOOD IS TOO GOOD!

$E = mc^2$ WILL DEFINE HOW THIS book will end.

Energy equals mass times the speed of light squared.

There is an immutable and unchallenged law in physics that has stood the test of time. It says that a corresponding mass will be maintained as a constant in any reaction in the universe. *Whatever amount you put in, anything that will create a reaction, you will end up with a sum interchangeably equal to what you put in.* Albert Einstein had explained it quite complicatedly, and it could be nauseous to the untrained. But then, woe to us, he was addressing his peers. So let me give you my take on it, certainly not from his peer level but from your average guy sitting at the back of your classroom.

Again, what you put in, you'll get a sum equal to that, and interchangeably as well.

If we are to go back to our little chairs after playing in the sandbox, it simply means that whatever letter in the alphabet we see on the board and put into our little brains on our first day in school will be the takeaway input. Then when we get home, as we show our pencil works to our mom, saying, "Mom, today, I've learned A, B, and C." we get something back. And that is what it is - what you see, you learn. What you learn, you share. What you share comes back to you. For the quick learning and the sharing with your mom, you get a kiss on the cheek – that is the reaction.

But why has life become so complicated?

If you're not color-blind, there are only three *primary* colors in this tapestry of life – Red, Yellow, and Blue.

But hey, look what Vincent Van Gogh did with those three colors when he mixed them – The Starry Night! Or look what Leonardo da Vinci came up with when he painted the Mona Lisa or the Sistine Chapel ceiling when Michelangelo Buonarroti was so animatedly inspired.

There are only twenty-six letters in the alphabet but look how the people in the world communicate with one another.

See how the twenty-six are interchangeably mixed to create misunderstanding and chaos. But also see how they have brought peace and freedom. "I declare war" uses only eleven letters. "Go, you're free," also has eleven. "God bless you" also has only eleven letters, but it has made people soar to heights in their earthly pursuits. In numerology, the number eleven is the gateway to enlightenment and spirituality.

In the movie Sound of Music, governess Maria teaches the Von Trapp children that they can sing only seven notes, starting with Do-Re-Mi.

Yes, only seven notes we can pin on the staff but look what these gentlemen did with those seven notes: Ludwig Van Beethoven wrote his greatest composition of all time – Symphony No. 3 - Eroica, which he dedicated to Napoleon Bonaparte as he celebrated his conquests across Europe; Frédéric Chopin's Nocturne in E flat major Op 9 No 2, or Antonio Vivaldi's The Four Seasons to name a few.

There are only ten numbers to start with: 1 to 10 but look what those numbers can do when you combine them all to create a computation.

Albert Einstein once said that the 8th wonder of the world is a mathematical computation called the Compounded Interest. He says that for those that understand it – earn from it, and for those that don't – pay it. And this has created a wide gulf between the rich and the poor in all nations. So, again just ten numbers to start with.

There are 3 million "pieces" of a NASA space rocket, and each one is so vital that if we say there is a 10 percent flaw, it will mean 300,000 pieces need to be looked into. So, again just the numbers 1 to 10 - and mathematics has never been the same.

There are only two greatest commandments in the Bible for man: Love thy neighbor as thyself and Love God with all thy heart, mind and soul. Simply put, two doctrines to follow: Love God and Love your neighbor.

But look what we've all become.

I am no physicist. I am no painter. I am not a poet or a statesman, neither am I a musician or a mathematician. But certainly, I understand what loving God and neighbor is, but here's the thing: It is just easier said than done.

So, let's simplify things.

We only need to do three simple things in life.

First, *always do good.*

Love begets love. In any relationship, what you put into it, you will reap. The Book of Hosea (760-720 BC) spoke about sowing and reaping. The wisdom of this adage has crossed the bar of scrutiny for thousands of years, finding its way even outside of the religious context. In 1822 it echoed in the halls of the British parliament when a speaker warned against the policies of England in its colonies – "What we sow, we reap."

I once spoke to a group of couples about marriage. At the outset, I gave a disclaimer saying that I was neither an expert on marriage nor a theologian specializing in holy matrimony. Still, I said I could only speak from experience. I said, "Marriage is like a box." People get married believing that everything they hope to find in life, is in this box– love, romance, stability, companionship, and fun, and these are tied to the deed of the marriage itself.

I said it was wrong. Marriage is like an empty box. You must put love, romance, stability, companionship, and fun into the box to get it back in refined form – for you and your partner. Inversely, if you can put good things in it, you can also throw in trash, like disrespect, infidelity, complacency, and the like. Garbage in – garbage out if we're talking computer jargon.

All told, if we want to have a life that is good, we have to do good in our life.

Let's talk about the war between the Hutus and the Tutsis in Rwanda, where about two million were murdered. Preceding this were years of animosity between the two ethnic groups. Still, the genocide was sparked in April 1994 when the plane carrying the presidents of Rwanda and Burundi was shot down. Even without the investigations, the Tutsis were blamed for it; after a few hours, the national radio was blasting a call to arms by the Hutus. A few months later, the Tutsi population was almost wiped out – by murder and forced evacuation.

Amid the gripping tension, enter a Holocaust survivor with a Ph.D. in Stanford who had been lecturing about genocide at Harvard University. Ervin Staub realized that there should be something that would put the groups back into reconciliation. When he researched the origins of the genocide, he found out that the call to arms by the most popular radio station in the country was instrumental in inciting hatred and moving the soldiers to make the killings.

He decided to use that same medium to bring back peace. He was unsure if it would work, but he knew it was a good start, although he believed the returns might be long-drawn. He was audacious and fearless.

With a group of Rwandan writers, they created a radio soap opera called *Musekeweya*. It was about a love story and eventual intermarriage of lovers from two warring ethnic tribes – clearly an allusion to the Hutus and Tutsis. It became so popular that the warring peoples related to the story. Every time the program ran on the radio, everyone stopped what they were doing and just listened.

Finally, in the last episode, when the main characters were to be married, the station's hotline was jammed with listeners asking that the marriage be done live on stage in a huge stadium so the whole nation could watch. What they found out in the months that followed was a revelation. Hutus and Tutsis were intermarrying despite their ethnic biases. Although this did not happen immediately, the seed that the Musekeweya planted bore fruit. The good that came out of individual intermarriages grew exponentially.

It is the same with goodness. Like a seed, someday it will bear fruit. Doing good is the only thing that will yield a result where everybody wins. A simple case of one plus one equals two ad infinitum. It is an example of the $E=mc^2$. Whatever you put in will equal what you take out.

The second thing to do is – *always speak goodness.*

The Musekeweya experiment scriptwriters ensured that the soap opera dialogues in the roles would always invariably speak of goodness. In your case, speaking good might get you a rebuke; people will ignore you; people will mistake it as a weakness and take advantage of you. You might get persecuted, but in the end, just like the sown seed, you will reap the kind you sow.

In this book, I have talked about my mother and the need for forgiveness to have a good finale in her life. Forgiveness held her hand gently on her deathbed. While it was ignored at first, the seed was sown.

The words we speak can make or break a person or a relationship. They will somehow define character whether these are said within life's vibrancy or on the deathbed. Throughout history, spoken words have sent millions to their freedom, some to their graves, and some to their greatness or downfall.

From Martin Luther King's "I have a dream" to John F. Kennedy's "We choose to go to the moon" speech at Rice University or the note by Harry Truman on July 31, 1945, saying "Release when ready" given at the Potsdam conference about the atomic bomb. All those words defined the paths of men.

History is replete with famous words of great men on the world stage or even in the solitary room of their deathbeds, like the following last words – from the hilarious to the humble, from the smart-alecky to the blunt:

Take Humphrey Bogart's "I should never have switched from scotch to martinis" or Leonardo da Vinci's "I have offended God and mankind because my work did not reach the quality it should have" after finishing his Mona Lisa. Or Jesus Christ's "Father, into thy hands I commend my spirit." Or Oscar Wilde's "Either that wallpaper goes, or I do." Or Steve Jobs' "Oh wow!" and Winston Churchill's "I'm bored with it all."

Somehow, those last words make us believe that men prodigiously want to communicate their inner thoughts up to their last breaths. From this premise, it should not be difficult to find the impetus in our resolve never to stop speaking to others until our final moments, if only to make the world a little better. This notwithstanding Karl Marx dousing all the literary attempts of the dying with his, "Last words are for fools who believed they have not said enough."

I still firmly believe that words, be they given on a fine day or the deathbed, *should be spoken if they are to bring out the good in everyone. An unspoken good word is one too many a missed opportunity at greatness.*

English conductor Benjamin Zander spoke of talking to an elderly woman who survived the Holocaust. With her 9-year-old brother, she was a 15-year-old older sister who was herded into a train bound for Auschwitz. With hundreds of other children who had lost their parents, they were cramped into crowded cars one wintry day. As she looked down, she found out that her brother was barefoot. After all the panic of the round-up, he had left his shoes. "How stupid of you! Why did you forget your shoes!" She scolded him so badly all the way to the concentration camp.

When they arrived, they were separated from each other, and she never saw him again.

She said that if she could only turn back the hands of time, she would only say kind words to her baby brother. And she made a vow "never to say anything that will stand as the last thing she would ever say."

For us, the living - always speak goodness as far as practicable. Create an infinite ripple.

Did you notice there is hardly any unkind word ever said in a eulogy? Why wait to speak goodness until the guy is dead? Every good word said on any day is a seed of goodness planted. Let us all remember that.

The third thing to do is *be significant.*

What do I mean by this?

Unless we are a shipwrecked long-bearded dude on a small island in the middle of an ocean, we are social animals.

Make a difference in another person's life. Be significant in somebody else's world. We are all interconnected in this great circuitry of life that, somehow, any goodness we exude will create a good vibe in others.

We do not need power, wealth, or fame to do this. We simply need to do our best in our little way when we connect with others. There is nothing more fulfilling than seeing people's eyes light up when they see you coming. Let them say to your face, "I am blessed to have you in my life."

It is not about coming into somebody else's life saying, "Hey, I 'm here; see what I can do!"

It is about, "Hey, I'm here; *how can I help?*"

On my first day in a large company years back, I looked hard into myself and asked that question.

On my last day when I left, I felt everyone was prepared to go to the next level.

St. John the Baptist said it aptly. "He must increase, while I must decrease."

If all of us wear scars

for every hurt and pain

in our life, we'd all be

unrecognizable in

the end.

Chapter Three

The Scars of Life

The Story of the Blue Winter Gloves

I love Friday nights in the summer.

On a loose routine, my boys, now grown up, would invite their mom and me to a night out at some area where we could eat take-out food. We'd unfold our picnic chairs stashed in our car trunks and go to an overly vast parking lot by some coffeehouse in Heartland Town Centre. Otherwise, it would be the half-moon concrete seats near a Subway deli not far from there.

With the usual 6-inch pizza sub and Popeye's mild chicken, we would chill out with sweet nothings until we'd feel the breeze get nippy.

One topic that always jumps up, skipping the line, would be the story of the blue winter gloves.

On our first winter in Canada together as a family, we stayed in a high-rise apartment building along Highway 10 in Mississauga. As I would later find out, all its tenants were new immigrants from all over – South Asia, the

Baltic, the Middle East, China, and the rest of Europe. And just like many, they had kids my boys' age.

Canada has a great immigrant support system. We would periodically get mail about what to do and where to go about the basics needed to get settled. We would get a brochure package - something like a survival kit that helps new immigrants where to get their health cards, where to get their academic credentials assessed, where to locate food banks to get free groceries and where to find a job closest to their qualifications.

I had signed up for job placement assistance at a Settlement Centre at the corner of Burnhamthorpe and Dixie Road. The lady at the counter asked me to fill out a form where they'd ask for all my details - short of a biography, so perhaps they could put me into a certain demographic class. I was in the jobless, indigent, and needy category.

That winter, as my 10-year-old twins were in the lobby waiting for the elevator, they saw a van drive up the main entrance. Two men unloaded boxes of what appeared to be Christmas presents. As the twins would later recount, it did not matter if it was toys or books as long as they were presents. It was Christmastime, and they were brimming with excitement.

Even when the gift boxes delivered to our front door did not appear to be toys, the boys were ecstatic. When they opened their presents on Christmas day, what they got will forever define how we all started our life in Canada – at least in their definition.

Both got oversized bright blue fluffy winter gloves, a Snakes and Ladders board game box, and a New York Yankees cap.

They rocketed to cloud nine.

Coming from a tropical country, wearing gloves was something unheard of. Perhaps the only gloves they'd be familiar with are the Manny Pacquiao boxing gloves. The blue gloves were going to be their new 'bragging rights' second to their bikes (which they picked up from the huge green trash bin at the back of the building).

They'd put the blue gloves on their tiny hands and jauntily walk around the apartment, even trying to grasp their forks and knives when they ate their breakfast. I thought I saw two Mickey Mouses with oversized gloves personified for a moment.

"I can't wait to go back to school after Christmas, Pa!" They exclaimed as they waved their gloved hands to my face, but I knew they wanted to brag.

True enough, as they dressed for the first day after the holidays, it was gloves first, even before the pants.

But when they got home later that day, it looked like a black hole had just sucked them in. There was a glum look on their faces as they slowly closed the door.

"Pa, about six other kids wore the same blue winter gloves!"

I said, "That's okay; at least all of you blue glovers could now band together and call yourselves the Band of Brothers!" That's me and my dark humor trying to beguile them. "Or they must be within this apartment too!" I was looking for a way out to appease their disappointed souls.

But seriously, I figured those kids also had dads who were jobless, indigent, and needy.

It's funny, but those blue winter gloves have now become symbolic of how we started our life in Canada.

Like a scar forever etched in us, the story about the gloves speaks of our early days, mainly untold until now. Yet we are all fondly reminded of where we started - definitive and endearing.

Scars often tell a great story. Let's look at the scars of the great American novelist Ernest Hemingway.

As a young man, he frequently injured himself in boyhood misadventures, football games, and schoolyard brawls. As a daredevil sportsman in boxing matches, bullfights in Pamplona, Spain, safari hunts in the African Serengeti, and deep-sea fishing in Bimini, he had all the bruises and scars much like our own badge of truth. As a war correspondent in the Spanish civil war and as a Red Cross ambulance driver in Italy, he was wounded by machinegun fire and mortar shells that missed him by a tent's radius. He survived two plane crashes (in two successive days in 1954) and three serious car accidents.

Everything said, his body was like a canvas of scars – all a testament to his adventures and what he went through in his life. The scars even found their way into his novels. In the Old Man and the Sea, he wrote about the cranky and steely fisherman Santiago whose "hands have the deep creased scars from handling heavy fish on the cords. But none of these scars were fresh. They were as old as erosions in a fishless desert."

Later, he would say, "Every man's life ends the same way. It is only the details on how he lived that distinguish one from the other."

If all of us wore scars on our faces for every hurt and pain, we'd all become unrecognizable. We'd all be like a walking declaration of battles lost and won. But let me tell you, there'd be respect and awe for everyone when we see the scars of what each one has gone through. Like military stripes, the more there are, the more battles fought. Same struggles, pains, and triumphs. Same failures. Life doesn't hand us everything on a silver platter. We have to become scarred and tattered to become real and to feel what true love is - just like the Velveteen Rabbit.

One of the best dialogues I've ever read was in a children's story – The Velveteen Rabbit, by Margery Williams. It was between the toys – Skin Horse and the Velveteen Rabbit. I want to quote a few of their conversations.

"Real isn't how you are made," said the Skin Horse. "It's a thing that happens to you. When a child loves you for a long, long time, not just to play with, but REALLY loves you, then you become Real."

"Does it hurt?" asked the Rabbit.

"Sometimes," said the Skin Horse, for he was always truthful. "When you are Real, you don't mind being hurt."

"Does it happen all at once, like being wound up," he asked, "or bit by bit?"

"It doesn't happen all at once," said the Skin Horse. "You become. It takes a long time. That's why it doesn't often happen to people who break easily or have sharp edges, or who have to be carefully kept. Generally, by the time you are Real, most of your hair has been loved off, and your eyes drop out, and you get loose in the joints and very shabby. But these things don't matter at all because once you are Real, you can't be ugly, except to people who don't understand."

In life, there will always be something that will remind you of your past. It could be a knee scar, a broken tooth, a limp, or anything. But beyond what we see with our naked eye are the scars within the soul. They are much more painful and difficult to heal. The wounds of the soul make you real.

The sum of all these things will define you. But let's all be aware that all the pains in the world are not only caused by the absence of love or the mere infliction of hate alone or by loss. Paradoxically, some hurts and pains are also caused by love for something else. It's confusing that people sometimes inflict pain in the name of love – or they think they do. And these things usually happen in couple relationships. All these will show that, at some point in your life, you loved and were loved – even with all the pain.

In the end, what heals everything ultimately is not only love and time. And why so? Because love may drag its feet and come slow, and time may take forever to move. What will work out healing will be your adaptability, your capacity to absorb pain and hurts, and how you react to it. Forgiveness, love, time, adaptability, and ability to absorb pain – all these things have to work together.

If scars were a symbol of Ernest Hemingway's life, for us, I'd say it would be the oversized blue winter gloves.

Inside the gift box with the gloves that Christmas was also the gift of Love between one another - long missed in *real presence* after we lived separately from each other. We did not realize it right away, but that box of gifts also brought us all back together.

And the blue gloves?

They always go well with the 6-inch pizza subs and Popeye's mild chicken.

What we become,

we experience first.

Chapter Four

Hyperthymesia

Google It!

Life is an avid collector of memories. It has Hyperthymesia.

Yesterday, as I was browsing through the LP disc records section of our neighborhood Value Village store (a cousin of the Salvation Army and Goodwill stores), I found a Sammy Kaye album called Popular American Waltzes. I remember we had this album back home, which is why the cover quickly caught my eye. It must have been the longing for the beautiful memories of my childhood that made me pick it up right away. As I reminisced over its cover design, I instantly harkened back to one of those warm evenings when as a child, I would watch my dad do a graceful waltz with my mom to a song in this album. Although they could do a slick and whippy Tango to a Perez Prado tune, the waltz was more definitive of their chemistry than the other genres.

Under the low-watt tri-colored cylindrical red, white, and green lamps that hang (still there today) from our high ceiling and to the tempo of Kaye's Tennessee Waltz and Diane, they would dance the night away on certain evenings as if it was a Friday night. She would dance barefooted, eyes shut, and side face gently pressed on my dad's breast, both starkly resembling a Xavier Cugat caricature of lovers intertwined like wrought iron in a tight embrace. I would see their sweat glisten on their foreheads as they'd swirl around like there was no tomorrow.

Whether it was the Johnnie Walker Red, the repressed love (restrained by their busy schedules) between them, or something called testosterone that guided their dancing moves is a mystery I would prefer die as a happy thought.

With his lighted Salem cigarette parked on the ashtray immolating itself into ash on the table, the living room would turn itself into a wee-hour barroom with heavy smoke overcast on a welter of discordant sounds. Bare feet swishing on the floor and the scratchy noise of the record player needle all mix to celebrate the moment. He'd hurriedly puff on his Salem between songs, never letting go of her hand. My younger sister Suzette and I would watch them glide blithely across the floor, all oblivious to the gaze of the little eyes. They would be lost in the moment until the long shadows of the night would take them by the hand to carry us to our bedrooms for the evening.

So yes, life is a collection of memories, and I'm sure you are recollecting yours with your folks as you read these lines. You can stop here, gaze up at your ceiling and reminisce; I don't mind.

When I played this album today, the memories evoked by the songs had me believe that perhaps the sentimental fool that I have turned out to be could be an offshoot of those great moments - all captured by such music, long asleep in the backroads of my imagination. *Indeed, what we become, we experience first.*

We are a constantly progressive sum of all our experiences. What we habitually do and do not do every day becomes what we are - and that's what makes up our life. But life is a collage too challenging to understand, just like an abstract painting. And just like the greatest paintings in the world, they are best understood and appreciated when we step back and gaze from a distance - that's why you have seats in the middle of art gallery halls and museums.

The person we become is a collection of our past triumphs, failures, mistakes, and all. But we don't have to be a prisoner of that past. We should constantly evolve into someone better than we were before. Ergo, our experiences today and how we deal with these all put together will define the person we become tomorrow, and the goal is always to become a better version of ourselves. There is no one else that possesses this power to change but us. Ralph Waldo Emerson says, *"What lies behind us and what lies before us are tiny matters compared to what lies within us."* We have all the art tools we need, so the work to reach perfection never ends. It is always a never-ending process until we die. We paint a picture of ourselves until our last breath.

All told, until we do our last paintbrush stroke, we remain an unfinished masterpiece. Nobody paints on our life's canvas except us. So, let's hold the brush firmly in our hands and not let anyone take it away. We have to make sure that when we paint our life, we paint it well so everyone, like the art auctioneer, in the end, can go on chasing after raised bids for our story.

Although you might be long gone to know its value and enjoy the proceeds, a reward somewhere awaits you. Only those left behind will one day look at your canvas and pass judgment. I would love to see them take a step back and say, "what a beautiful picture my dad has painted about his life."

But of all the greatest things to hear, there'd be only one that would matter after all – *"Well done, my good and faithful servant. You have been faithful with a few things; I will put you in charge of many things. Come and share in your master's happiness!"* (Matthew 25:21)

When you paint your life, do the things that speak of who you are. Surely all the good that we are and can become can only come from the Source of all goodness. The one thing I can say you'll never go wrong is to be true to yourself. And why do I say this? It is because your true self is a reflection of your Maker.

The You that reflects everything about yourself and your life is the real picture that will stand out because no one is like you. Like a fingerprint, you are unique. Even my identical twins Lorenzo and Leandro have separate and distinct ways and personalities only peculiar to one despite their uncanny likeness. So, whatever you do, follow your heart's path. When you do this, the lines, curves, and colors will all fall naturally into place.

Rapper JZ says, "Remind yourself that nobody's built like you. You design yourself."

Steve Jobs once said," Remembering I'll be dead soon is the most important tool I've ever encountered to help me make the big choices in life. Because almost everything – all external expectations, all pride, all fear of embarrassment or failure – these things fall away in the face of death, only leaving what is truly important. Remembering that you will die is the best way to avoid the trap of thinking you have something to lose. You are already naked. There is no reason not to follow your heart." You lose nothing when you do good and stay good. Staying good is always a win-win situation, although one doesn't get the prize immediately.

Every day of our life is a brushstroke drawn by our hand, and how the montage appears will depend on how the lines, curves, and colors are mixed and drawn. While I expect some turbulence in the strokes, there will always be grace when the curves and colors connive. When we put on the face of anger, hatred, indifference, and all those detestable lot, the strokes turn dismal, turning the picture dull and dreary. But when we are happy and kind, the whole picture lights up with the brightest colors.

While imperfections will get in the way, redemption by grace in our choices will always be a generous buffet and will all be there for the taking.

After all, life has never been a straight line. Never diametrical. Never monochromatic. And while they say life is a circle, it is never perfect. Never has been, never will be.

The passage of time turns life experiences into great works of art. How these experiences influence one will dictate the movements of the hand strokes and the choice of colors on the palette. Let us remind ourselves that life is an art, and God is the sole and ultimate connoisseur. As each day plays before your very eyes, so will your hand that holds the paintbrush on the canvas. There are almost 8 billion people today; each is a unique masterpiece, no matter their circumstances. In God's eyes, each has an art value and a great story to tell his generation.

So, no matter how bad and darkly overcast your day will be, you still have a choice. You are the one holding the palette. You are the one holding the paintbrush. The colors are yours for the picking. You can always put bright colors and lightness in your strokes, regardless.

Even in his struggles and infirmities, Vincent Van Gogh made the stars swirl and dance in the darkest nights, and the barren and dreary wheatfields burst to life.

So can you.

Life's end is not a

matter of choice.

What to do about it is.

Chapter Five

Life, Death, and Taxes - your call

My mother used to tell me, "There is nothing in life surer than death and taxes."

I believe her.

People may get around taxes, skim them, dodge them, park them, or pay them. But death is straightforward, no frills, and at times blunt.

But let's not talk about taxes. Let our accountants handle that. For now, let's talk about life and death.

But first, Life.

Many of us are outrageously disconnected from the relationship between life and death. Philosophers Socrates, John Locke, and the religious would say everyone has a right to life. For a brief time in history, not too long ago, they found allies in the legalists when the philosophy finally found its way enshrined in the constitution - The right to life, liberty, and property – up until Roe versus Wade created the stir.

Today, there is a fiercely contested war about who decides who lives and who dies; perhaps it will never end. It might even worsen as the world descends into increased idolatry of the Self. The armies of contention continue to go to war with their boots over the carcasses of defenseless little ones. How this will go in the future will be a guess that'll get good as it gets. And all this because they could not agree about when life begins and when life is wanted or unwanted. We have become gods in some way, I guess.

But so much for that. Let's talk about life for us, the living, because that's what I intended this book to be about, and then death, briefly as you read on.

We were never promised that our existence on earth is assured. Our days have never been guaranteed. Like a car, there'll be a guaranty and lots of warranties. But for life, the guaranty is that there is no guarantee. While there are thousands of warranties presented, they cannot warrant extending life. Life's expiry is final.

Sure, there are warranties on where to find healing, where to find happiness in case of breakdowns, where to find comfort in case of pain, and so on. And they're all either biblical or secular. But regardless, somebody has to switch off your lights one day, and no warranty can ever stop that.

So, nobody knows the exact time and day we step out of the Big Door. And that, to me, is the beauty of life.

Emily Dickenson, on Life, says matter-of-factly," That it will never come again is what makes life so sweet." It is why we hug loved ones tight – we're afraid we might not have the chance to do it again. The pleasant suspense of not knowing when it ends makes the present moment more meaningful. This adds weight, therefore, to the words of the wise – do not live in the past nor the future but in the moment. Winston Churchill succinctly says, "If we open a quarrel between past and present, we shall have lost the future."

Because if our life here on earth were promised to be forever, we'd take it for granted.

And there are people today who are precisely doing that. They think and act like they've got a Permanent Resident Card (yes, it's the PR Card for you Canadians) on Earth. They don't give a toss about relationships, who's getting hurt and robbed of dignity, and acting like the here and now is all that matters. Plain hubris, but that's them.

If we only put value on the belief that tomorrow is never promised, we'd change the way we live. We'd rethink how we use our time and energy and not sweat the small stuff. We'd say "I Love You" as often as we get the chance or say "I'm Sorry" without overthinking. If we think that today is our last day on planet Earth, chances are we will do the things we need to do with all our hearts, souls, and minds. You'd do that, won't you?

Now, let's talk about death.

J.R.R. Tolkien talks about it in The Fellowship of the Rings. "I wish it need not happen in my time," said Frodo. "So do I," said Gandalf. "...and so do all who live to see such times. But it is not for them to decide. *We must decide what to do with the time given.*"

I have a friend who recently passed away. He would have been 56 this year, but cancer took him away. He was first diagnosed two years ago by a doctor who was straightforward with him, saying he'd live for two months at the most. He was stocky and always bubbly, which could be why the doctor felt he could take the blow. But he was soft within. Soft for young children and old friends. His endearment to children was phenomenal, and my 12-year-old granddaughter Maia would remember him with fondness every time she'd hear us pray for him.

While I would say he was strong in the sense that he'd thumb down his nose at the disease – it was his faith in God that kept his hope of getting healed. Not even his pain could squeeze his spirit dry.

He lived for two more years after that diagnosis. Gradually over his terminal years, he became more aware that his days were numbered and that the existential part of his life was *no longer a choice*, yet his hopes were still high. What remained a matter of choicc to him was how he felt toward the remaining time before him. He chose only one formidable course of action through all that was happening – *to believe.* Confucius once said that "healthy men want a thousand things, but a sick man only wants one."

As time passed, his options narrowed to two non-negotiable things: To love and serve the Lord.

His feelings toward life and its creator were taken to a new level. *What he* ***decided*** *to do with his remaining days became a turning point.* Note that I am using the word "decided," which is an action word.

As I said, he chose to remain faithful to his calling to love and serve the Lord despite all his sufferings. Even with mobility issues, he decided to allow friends and relatives to come and visit together by just being where he was in his sorry state, where he'd know they'll all come to see him. He lit up the lives of those troubled with the anxiety of not knowing how to live their day-to-day lives by just showing them how to take the blows. In all his debilitating condition, he showcased serene grace. His mere passive presence alone became a symbol of silent strength and faith.

Ironically, the able-bodied friends who flocked to his side in his most vulnerable and pathetic moments had looked up to him to draw the strength they could not find in them and could only wish they had. He became a powerful image of how to keep the faith in the worst of times. What he did or did not do defined his resolve to push his dedication to the hilt under such extreme pain.

Now that's one heck of a legacy.

To know that one day, somebody will switch off your lights is an astonishing truth that will make you love life and understand that life is worth living. Knowing that your loved ones and friends will suffer the same fate as you makes you even more motivated to value their company every moment you get and not take them for granted.

It makes you value each millisecond of your time – and lets you sort out the difference between the ones you need to sweat out and those that don't deserve your while.

Journalist Chuck Palahniuk once said this: "We all die. The goal is not to live forever, but to create something that will."

Well, somebody I know just did that.

Incidentally, his name is also Chuck.

If you're telling me you're

not good at anything, then

you've really not searched

hard into yourself.

Chapter Six

In Life, We Tire but Not Retire

I RETIRED LAST YEAR. **It was my third.** I first retired when I was 38.

I worked for the biggest, the best, and oldest bank until I got a call one day inviting me to join a competing bank that wanted to be the biggest and the best - never mind oldest because this one was 111 years younger. I left with a handsome package and toured abroad before starting my new job.

If Simon Sinek says that most CEOs agree that employees come first in the hierarchy of values to achieve growth over profitability and shareholder value, I'm flattered (lol). A year after I joined the new bank (yes, the younger one), it became number one in assets when it merged with another big one. If employees are indeed considered assets, this was a time to be delusional.

I worked there with the best out-of-the-box thinkers on the corporate planet. But as employees were getting younger and more daring, I was getting old and more circumspect – a crossing of the demographics line in the coordinate plane of life. 13 years later and a step from the top, I retired and made the great move to Canada. And this was my second retirement.

But that was 14 years ago.

I did my 3rd retirement last year (ho-hum) after returning from my Camino de Santiago pilgrimage walk in Spain. While there, I emailed my superiors my letter of retirement. After some deep soul-searching and a hundred thousand steps across the vast Galician region, I felt that my feet were more at home in my worn-out sandals than in my Pradas. Working in banks and financial institutions for more than 30 years was enough to expunge all the numbers from my head but the zero digit. I felt that another year after our benefits and pension fund company was bought by Goldman Sachs was too long for a weary and dulled old man. Besides, I feared making more monumental gaffes than the epic ones I already did.

And I thought it was time to see the world in my mid-Anacapa Gore-Tex shoes. There was the dream of a small house by the sea in a quaint town in New Brunswick and enjoying the sunset. There was the 9-day Marangu Route to Mt Kilimanjaro in Tanzania and a doable 15-day trek to Annapurna base camp towards Mt. Everest. My wife says it's more wishful talk pumped enough to explode a delusional old dreamer's body. Well, the last time I checked, dreams were still free.

But a month after all the dreaming, I was asked to lead a non-profit organization called the Brotherhood of Christian Businessmen and Professionals. Cool.

All of a sudden, I shrunk. I felt incapable, undeserving, and not up to the task by any measure. The 3-year term was going to be longer than the walk from St-Jean Pied de Port at the Pyrenees to Santiago de Compostela, more formidable than the Annapurna Base Camp, and more strenuous than the African trek.

I had a plethora of excuses all stacked under my sleeve, ready to come out if they would insist. I was a senior. I am only good at talking to myself, not with others; I had memory lapses and just wanted to walk around in my flip-flops - enjoy bohemian life and see the world.

But after a long and deep invocation of the 3-in-1 God, I could not bail out, bluff my way off the card table. Through sleepless nights, I had asked the Lord to give me the wisdom to accept that the only difference between the Yes and the No was not the old man's body but the unwilling spirit and that the only way for the Yes to win was for humility and gratitude to kick in. My soul wanted to give back and say thank you to the God who's given me some of the greatest blessings in the world I don't even deserve. In a brief moment of prayer, I simply accepted that I'd be nothing without God's help. It is His work, and I'll be a worker at His beck and call.

When I finally said yes and did my acceptance speech, I said that if I believe that I cannot do it, then I am relying on my mortal power and strength – and that means I am not putting God into the equation, not allowing Him to show what He can do through me. It was all about faith in what God can do and not what I can and cannot do.

Today, I could easily be a bored panda, slouching the day away in my backyard.

But I watch in awe at how God works things out - not my way but His way. While so many glitches are thrown with the pandemic's effects, I remain calm and almost laissez-faire knowing that God takes the wheel.

I begin the day with a simple prayer asking God to help me live through the hours peacefully and safely for myself, my family, and others. I pray for the sick, the departed and the difficult people I meet daily. I then review a list of the other things I need to do for the day. Surprisingly, besides the prayers, I usually end up not accomplishing anything except for a seven to ten-kilometer walk before taking a nap.

My kids are infuriated whenever they see me still in bed at ten in the morning, not eating the right foods and exercising. Finding the right motivation to get up from bed on any given day for one who's retired can be like forcing yourself to wake up early on a Sunday morning. It seems like I badly need the motivation to find the motivation.

As we grow older, there is a disconnect between what we need to do and what we just lazily allow to flow unproductively out of our day. I call this the motivation void. If there is no motivation, there is no way to start what you're supposed to do.

In her song Ironic, Alanis Morissette says, "Life has a funny way of sneaking up on you." During the years that I was working, the motivation to wake up, rise, and go was dictated by things *without me* – my boss, the tardiness memo, the HR reprimand, the pink slip, the motivation to get a raise and a promotion. But now that the motivation resides solely *within me*, it's suddenly gone.

Dr. Seuss says,

"You have brains in your head. You have feet in your shoes.

You can steer yourself in any direction you choose

You're on your own. And you know what you know

And you are the one who'll decide where to go."

There lies the irony. When we were not given the power to make our own decisions, we were motivated to move. And when we finally have the power to decide, independent of external forces, we suddenly lose the motivation to move. I don't get it. If there's a reason for all this nonsense, it's a whole science.

Our mayor in Mississauga, Hazel McCallion, served in office for more than 40 straight years. She'd win 12 elections straight. Nobody could beat her. She served under 8 Canadian Prime Ministers and retired when she was 93. I've seen her walk during town parades, and she'd come to the office driving alone.

When asked what kept her working for so long, she said, "I don't know what I'd do. I want to keep myself busy. There are still challenges."

Challenges are what keep us moving. Even the most peace-loving guy you know will step up, ready to pounce on you when he's challenged. Challenges are motivations, and we need them to make us move.

The Okinawans hold the record of having the greatest number of centenarians in the world. National Geographic says that in the village of Ogimi on this small island of Okinawa, there is a stone marker with scant wording in Japanese. It reads, "at 80, you are merely a youth. At 90, if your ancestors invite you to heaven, ask them to wait until you're 100, and you might consider."

So, what is their secret?

They have a word for it. *Ikigai.*

It means *'your reason for being* or *'why you get up in the morning.'*

There are four (4) components of Ikigai.

1. What do you love to do? What is it that you get a kick out of? Your Ikigai should be something that you enjoy doing. What is your passion? What is it that makes your heart sing?

2. What are you good at? If you tell me you're not good at anything, you've not searched hard within yourself. Finding out what gift you have will lead you to your Ikigai.

3. What can you get in return? What can you get rewarded for? It could be money to some, recognition to others, love and

compassion returning to you in a circle, or simply the inner joy of doing it. Go figure.

4. Once you've found it, ask yourself if the world needs it. Oh yes, what the world needs now is love – but that's taken. Be original. Find something new.

So, what is it that makes you rise in the mornings?

Isn't visualizing yourself dancing with your granddaughter on her wedding day not enough motivation for you?

Isn't seeing your children having a great family life down the road not reason enough?

Isn't visualizing yourself with your loved one on a dock by the lake at sunset not reason enough to get up in the morning?

Isn't seeing yourself raise your trekking poles shouting, "I made it!" on top of Mount Kilimanjaro in Africa or at the Everest Base Camp in Nepal not enough for you?

Isn't realizing that God loves you and showers you with His blessings despite your failures and wayward ways not enough reason for you to wake up in the morning and give Him a profusion of your praise and thanks?

Seriously, think about it. What is your ikigai?

What motivates you?

You can run from

Philosophy 101

but you'll miss

all the fun.

Chapter Seven

You Are a Philosopher (You Just Don't Know It!)

When I was in my Philosophy 101 class, what were quite serious discussions sometimes turned out to be hilarious ones, with the mnemonics of syllogism thrown around the classroom like instruments of war between idiots. We'd laugh and repeat the words and laugh and repeat the words and make faces - *Bocardo, Darapti, Disamis, Datisi*. Behind our lady professor's back, as she wrote those words on the board, papers flew around as we rolled on the floor.

But seriously.

Philosophy is such a beautiful subject. It has a character of its own that explains why we are happy and why we are sad. Why we become angry, and why we become jubilant. Why our Friend Request has been ignored, and why we are unfriended on Facebook. Why our friend has suddenly come out from reticence to become the Selfie King. Why our lifeless and stoic teenage neighbor suddenly twerks on TikTok. Why our neighbor who lives in a shanty is much happier than a friend who has five cars in his garage. Philosophy is a whole universe of its own. Majestic like the stars but mysterious like nebulae. Wonderful like the twirling galaxies but scary like the Black Hole. Fairness and equality have a thousand and one definitions, depending on where you sit – and that's the mystery of Philosophy.

Emotions are movers of men. They take you where you allow them to take you, sometimes with your full consciousness and consent and sometimes not tacitly, like rage fueled by blind passion. Anger is a stubborn child who will lead you far from your usual self, perhaps even farthest from your boundaries of decency if uncontrolled. To be angry at anything, your mind, by instinct, either confronts the reason for the anger or walks away from it. Either way, the body, like a loyal soldier, follows the heart and mind. Experiential dualism might say the contrary (as in you might be in a precariously unpleasant position but is cheerful and confident, or you might still be the saddest guy even if the zaniest clowns surround you), but what will move the body to follow the heart and mind in either way will be plain audacity, or stupidity depending on the outcome. To move into action and follow what the heart says will always be a bold move. If this sounds philosophical, let me tell you now that it is. So, let's go back a bit to Philosophy 101.

The philosophy of the mind and the philosophy of truth is such a vast universe to be fully understood, unfathomable from our small orbit of understanding; it's so nuanced by different positions and theories of the world's greatest philosophers. To say that each of us may be influenced by their views is an understatement, but yes, we are. But it can also be the opposite, with us actually influencing their thinking long since time began. Either way, I digress. The reason is simple. Their philosophy was formed and influenced by their own experiences; therefore, it will always be relative. Out of this argument is that each of us picks up a little philosophy here and a little philosophy there; we then piece these all together and come up with our own according to how we see fit in our life.

In the end, the only philosophy applicable to you would be your own. Given all the circumstances around you, how you evolve into the person you were meant to be will form your philosophy. How you were raised, where you got your education, what norms you are comfortable with, who you interacted with, how people treat you, who you look up to, what makes you happy the most, and all those lot. In other words, you uniquely design your own sense of life.

Ultimately, who you turn out to be will become your unique philosophy. Right now, I run the risk of scorn by my sanctimonious friends for espousing a philosophy of the Self. But no, far from it. All I am doing is putting you in the middle ground of everything in your life, where you can have a 360-degree perspective, and certainly not in the corner of Ayn Rand, whose philosophy says that Self-Interest is the standard of morality and to see oneself as an end unto itself).

Let us remember that Free Will wears a neutral color – which puts you right smack between your existential self and God. And mysteriously, God has intentionally allowed that to happen. Because no matter His invitation to you to take His hand while you take your sweet time, you are still free to decide on your own.

This is why you are your own philosophy.

When you hit a wall,

sharpen your resolve.

It will cut through steel.

Chapter Eight

Two Stories. One Question.

If man had more animal than human in his dimensional existence, it would have been as simple as spear-hunting for food to survive and looking for cover to survive when hunted. He will be the hunter or the prey, depending on his position, strength, and vulnerability.

But man is a complex being. Aside from his raw survival needs, a wide array of drivers move him to action. He now has a whole spectrum of emotions to feed, varying from anger on one end to love on the other. In between, you'll find fear, pride, sadness, joy, desperation, confidence, and much more.

So, let me ask you.

Aside from surviving, what drove you to where you are today?

Was it your resolve to climb out of your dark hole? Did you run away from something wishing never to go back? Was it to amass more material wealth and win some more? Was it to find yourself? Was it to escape hurt and peel away resentment that may have almost thickened you to atrophy? Was it anger? Was it ambition? Was it because of fear of failure? Was it to prove something, and was it for yourself or others?

Whatever it is, your answer is your share and part of the equation. The other part was God's share. The equation of both has put you where you are today. And wherever that is, He wants you to know that in your assigned spot, all persons, places, and things will connive in time and space to glorify Him. And whether you like it or not, you are a part of a grand scheme. You are essential no matter how small your role is in the totality of things. Without you, the world will limp on its axis and be sadder, becoming much lesser than it is.

You may not see the wisdom right away - not now, or maybe even never. But the truth is, you are where you will do some good. Maybe not to you but to someone else. Somebody out there has a better life because of you, or you may have become a better you because someone out there has touched your life. Good will always come out of it simply because our God, who is the god of all goodness, has put you there.

Wherever God puts you, it is the exact place at the precise time. He wants you to grow there, seek Him, and reach out to Him in all moments. God puts you into a series of situations and events, leading to more situations and events to finally show you how great and mighty He is.

I have a friend from one of the islands down south in the Philippines called Siquijor. It is fabled as the hotbed of voodoo dolls and witches on flying broomsticks. However, such a reputation is now overtaken by tourism owing to the beauty of its pristine landscapes and white beaches.

His name is Etchin. It sounds like a Russian name, but no, he's not Russian. He is simply a guy who walked through life, walls, emptiness, and countless roadblocks. And all this feat because his vision was clear and sharp as a laser. Lasers, when focused, can cut through steel. But more than the laser focus that he had, his resolve was implacable.

I remember him talking about an incident when he was seven years old. A commotion woke him in the middle of the night with a heated argument between a relative and his father.

"Why force them to school when you cannot afford it? "He heard the relative scold his dad. They had run to him for help before classes started after summer.

Indeed, how can a lowly farmer, carpenter, and a plain homemaker afford to send nine children to school, let alone lift them from the pit of hardship?

As he heard his folks cry out to God in helplessness that night, his resolve to claw out of poverty saw its birth. Oh yes, births and pains have a never-ending love affair.

Today, that memory still haunts him.

Together with his siblings, they were forced to migrate to the big city, relegating their way as working students to university. With true grit, they fought for their scholarships until they succeeded.

God used a simple spark of an event, a humbling moment in that unforgettable night, to drive everyone in that tiny house to their limits and their unique spots in life.

While they were forced to train their sights with desperate hope far into the horizon beyond the seven coconut trees surrounding their old house, what they incidentally discovered was something right in front of their very eyes - the seven coconut trees.

The seven coconut trees were just enough to qualify his father to become a member of the Coconut Federation of the Philippines. Members of this federation get a shot to apply for a scholarship for their children.

Etchin became an accountant and married a brilliant wife who was also an accountant, and the rest, as they say, is history. After accounting for all he had been blessed with, he decided to give full credit where he saw it due. He returned the favor by paying forward with a mantra of sound ethics and honesty in his business dealings. Indeed a balanced book of one who has an unlimited escrow of gratitude.

Today he runs a corporation that is the number one taxpayer in the Philippines' customs brokerage industry.

When doors are shut to your face, and you seem to face a blank wall, look again.

No, not at the door, but inwardly into your soul.

If you find a tiny spark of hope in there, fan it.

Feed it.

Be angry but take courage.

St. Augustine once said, *"Hope has two beautiful daughters; their names are Anger and Courage. Anger at how things are, and Courage to see that they do not remain as they are."*

So, making it through from Siquijor, the poor boy did not soar to heights on a broom but in the simple godly gifts of hard work, honesty, and sheer faith in God.

As I recall this story, I am reminded of Robert Frost's words, "The best way out is always through."

And this boy just went through - through walls and his limits.

So, again, what drove you to where you are right now?

Well, my next story will be about a boy who made it through life literally through the broom. See if you can figure out what drove him. Since he's dead and can't answer the question, I'll do it for him instead.

It was 1943.

British prime minister Neville Chamberlain once said, "In war, whichever side may call itself the victor, there are no winners, but all are losers."

Motherland Philippines was embroiled in a war, not her own. So, she was a victim - and just like the people that loved her and would die for her, all were victims one way or the other.

The boy was 13 years old when he accompanied his distraught mother one morning as they rushed out of their nipa shack. His father had not returned for a few days after being invited by guerilla soldiers. Trudging sloshy on the muddy ground some kilometers eastward in Misamis Oriental Philippines, they feared the worst. When his white horse found its way back into their yard, they felt it was a harbinger they shuddered even to think about. The word was that travelers found a decomposing corpse along a Carabao path in a shallow grave.

It was the boy's father, Pedro. Shot at point-blank range at the back of the head by summary execution, his hand stuck out of a hurriedly dug grave as heavy rain had washed away dirt from the pit. He was suspected of being a spy for the Japanese soldiers by unfriendly locals whose dialect he did not speak and whose local customs he was unfamiliar with. He was among many migrants from Luzon who the locals did not favorably look upon but as invaders out to take away their land and opportunities. He was called "*Tagalog*" (a local dialect of the people of the Philippine Island of Luzon) by the local folk who did not know his first name. The man was the town treasurer who paid salaries in Japanese currency. Court records would say that the killers did not believe he loved his country and had questioned his nationalism.

He was an elementary school teacher and town treasurer who only had a few friends, not being homegrown. But he was diligent, industrious, and unassuming, just like your typical civil servant in the background who neither had the power nor the discretion - more so in this instance where everyone during this time of war was under a belligerent regime.

His son, the eldest of six siblings, bore the brunt of it all. To move beyond the grief, he had to embrace the reality that there was nothing he could do in his situation, in that place, at that time.

Angry and helpless but with courage, he ran away with his cousin Jose O. Castro, a boy his age. Hiding in the cargo hold of a ship to the Visayas, a group of islands midway to Luzon, the runaway boys took another boat to Manila.

In Manila, the boys worked as janitors during the day and went to school at night. The boy mopped and broomed floors at the halls of the Philippine House of Congress at night; alternately, during the day worked at the Philippine-American Cemetery transferring cadavers of GI soldiers, lining up the crosses, and running errands for a benevolent Secretary of Agriculture, Cesar Fortich. Their hard work paid off when they both finished university.

Jose O. Castro became a certified accountant, worked for a Manila bank and rose to become its president and CEO.

The orphaned boy finished his law studies and became a lawyer. But his jubilation was second only to his resolve to seek the truth about his father's death. Fresh from the bar, it was among his first few cases. With a damnably dogged persistence, he was able to piece together all the evidence, even with the lapse of time and all.

In the end, the Court's verdict was that his father was innocent of the suspicions – more a victim of war's atrocities like thousands of others. The dispositive part of the magistrate's judgment finally sent the poor man's soul to rest - and the killers to jail. A national daily, the Manila Chronicle called it "Case of the Year."

Beyond the retribution gained was the feeling of vindication. Don't we all desire peace in our hearts as we go about our daily life? Indeed, isn't it that what we simply ask of life is just to be kind to us, to live fair, happy, and long?

Our childhood may not be pleasant, but we don't have to be chained to that memory. Like lasers, we must cut through, broom through, and work our way out with whatever it takes. While our minds may be our greatest prison walls, they also hold the escape door – but only if we dare to and only if we gather the courage to break free. It is never too late to correct our unhappy childhood, even late in life.

So, the next time you need to go somewhere, sharpen your resolve, and you will cut through steel.

Just like in the first story, this boy had one resolve that clearly defined his direction. The apostle Paul had this kind of laser focus. Paul trained his sights so hard on spreading the good news by overcoming everything that stood in the way until the end.

Sometimes what keeps us from our goals are not the obstacles set by others but by us when we put limits on what we can do. Fear, complacency, and wrong motivations sometimes work as a ruthless team and create more enormous roadblocks to stop us. God always seems to put everything that's good on the other side of fear. The challenge is to cross the line relentlessly with steely grit.

The orphaned boy went through the thickest walls of odds and improbabilities to find delayed justice. And his steely resolve moved him to reach out for his dreams. The distance between dreams and reality is just two words: *Persistence and Boldness.* The poet Johann Wolfgang von Goethe once said, "whatever you can do, or dream you can, begin it. Boldness has genius, power, and magic in it."

So, the killers said his father had no nationalism?

They did not know the man well.

They did not even know what his children's names were. They did not know that he had named each one of them after the islands in the Philippines:

Luzonia, Visayo, Mindanao, Filipinas, Prosperidad and Lualhati (means Peace). Patently Filipino names, I tell you.

How can you get more nationalistic than that? If only they had checked the birth certificates.

Mindanao (Minding) was my father.

And he cut through steel.

There are three things

we mortals ever want to hear:

Mother, Home and

Heaven.

-William Goldsmith Brown

Chapter Nine

Mother

If I were to recall something very recent that would speak of how important mothers are, it would be a movie.

Saving Private Ryan.

The other day, for the umpteenth time, I watched it. I love that scene where General George C. Marshall, informed that Mrs. Ryan's three sons had been killed almost simultaneously within a few days of each other, read a letter by Abraham Lincoln to a group of army officers huddled around him. The letter was addressed to a widow, Lydia Parker Bixby of Massachusetts. Towards the middle part of the letter, General Marshall recited it without reading, perhaps indicating that it was close to his heart.

Mrs. Bixby had lost five sons in the Civil War. The handwritten letter was dated 21 November 1864. It was hand carried by a soldier to her from the Executive Mansion in Washington. Here's the text of that letter, verbatim:

Dear Madam,

I have been shown on the files of the War Department a statement of the Adjutant General of Massachusetts that you are the mother of five sons who have died gloriously on the field of battle. I feel how weak and fruitless it must be any word of mine which should attempt to beguile you from the grief of a loss so overwhelming, but I cannot refrain from tendering you the consolation that may be found in the thanks of the republic they died to save.

I pray that our Heavenly Father may assuage the anguish of your bereavement and leave you only the cherished memory of the loved and lost and the solemn pride that must be yours to have laid so costly a sacrifice upon the altar of freedom.

Yours very sincerely and respectfully,

Abraham Lincoln.

All over the film, the word Mother could be heard. In hushed conversations of the soldiers during lulls, in screams and cries of the dying, through the muddied lips of the infantryman on the beach in Omaha. The movie is replete subliminally at times, with scenes focusing on the tragedies of motherhood. There was the scene where the typist collected all the letters from different mail trays from different tables for Mrs. Ryan to be given to the War Department; There was the soldier who held his bloody guts screaming "Mama!"; there was the Giovanni Ribisi hushed conversation about his regrets not seeing his mother before leaving for the front. There was the poignant scene of Mrs. Ryan slumping to the ground upon seeing a military chaplain alight from his car by their porch. Steven Spielberg must've had great memories of his mother and loved her so much.

And here is where I come in.

Yes, I love my mother too.

My mother, Marie Lou Denosta, was born to a poor family who neither had the influence nor the money to wield through their existence. Her biological mother, orphaned at four, was a seamstress for an American orphanage in Bukidnon. Her father was a World War II veteran with nowhere to go after the war but the farm. The only weight they could throw around was the burden of raising a dozen children. Marie Lou (Mimi) was the eldest of six boys and six girls. Let's just say that siring twelve children was an economic strategy - as they say; it is always cheaper by the dozen. And let's also say that at a time when there was no electricity on their farm in Bukidnon, her dad made sure that kerosene expense (to light the lamp at night) was going to be the least in the budget if at all because he had much to do when the sun goes down. Well, twelve children will speak for that. *Res Ipsa Loquitor*. The thing speaks for itself.

Although she was later adopted, as was her sister, by her unmarried aunt, who was a daughter of the province's first governor, she remained close to her biological siblings.

She was a grade one teacher at the Xavier Ateneo. She could have taught music as she had the degree for it, but she preferred to teach young children.

The alphabet was much easier to teach than Frederic Chopin's Étude in E Major, Opus 10 No. 3 (Tristesse). Why do I make it difficult for you (lol) - it's popularly known as "No Other Love."

Perhaps, to de-stress herself coming home from her class where the 1 + 1 always gets the answer 11, she'd rather lose herself on the piano. The crescendo and legato of her left-hand haunt me to this day as I'd listen to her in the mornings while I ate my breakfast. This étude is such a beautiful song, and Chopin said it is his most beautiful composition. Every time I hear this song, it transports me back in time to our old house with her on the piano - just as Chopin himself was transported while listening to his student Adolf Gutmann play it for him. He rose from his seat, clasped his hands, and exclaimed, "How I miss my homeland, Poland." Now I rise, clasping my hands and say, "How I miss her."

The last time I saw her was when I left for Canada in January 2011 after my son's wedding in Cebu City. I stayed in Cagayan de Oro for only three days, having had to grapple with inane things I should have deferred for a time with her, now still bugging me as a guilt-laden afterthought. After the wedding, other small stuff stole my time away from her. She died two years later.

Looking back, I should have stayed longer with her. Time with a loved one should always be on top of the list, no matter what. I only stayed overnight with her preferring to stay at some hotel. Life is short, and time with someone who has infirmities may even quickly deny that chance.

Deep into the night, we spent time together talking like God had canceled tomorrow, finally hushing whispers into the wee hours. Great memories of people she came across were playfully painted in our conversations like a child's colorful collage. We pored over old photographs in her photo album. I saw how she kept little keepsakes of her stint as a teacher. There were bundled rubber bands of many colors, a broken Coca-Cola yoyo, a cracked and pockmarked spin top, and a few marbles. There were the flattened soda tin caps held together by wire. All those child trinkets were close to her heart simply because they brought beautiful memories of her students. Whenever I'd come home from a long absence, I'd open her huge antique chest where she kept all her photo albums, love letters, and a thousand and one things. Old letters and faded diaries, sepia photos, and dog-eared piano pieces always got the better of the curious cat in me. But I was always confidently assuring myself that satisfying my thirst for family memories would bring back the kill if it happened and would even be a hundred times worth it.

When she finally passed away after that visit, we regretted not being there more than we wished we had been when she was still alive. What I believe was heavier for her to carry than her debilitated body was not the physical pain but the burden of loneliness and the gnawing pain of yearning for the embrace of her children, who had all gone away to live in the United States and Canada. After all the persuasions and enticements for her to join us abroad, she chose to remain on her saggy couch. But we have long ago resigned ourselves to the thought that some things in life were meant to be and that they happen to give lessons to be learned. And this we admit with great remorse, even as we still carry this burden heavily in our souls. She died in 2013 without anyone of us, her children, by her bedside. From this sad episode, we have learned so much. Today, we earnestly hope and pray that destiny will be kinder to us.

But we have also learned that love, no matter the separation by distance, will always be a thought away and that a sigh whispered to the heavens can always bridge the gaping void of yearning for the love of family. Heaven has a way of distracting you away from your troubles. I am not offering any excuse for our absence but let me assure her, wherever she is right now, that love, all told, lives in the heart – and she knows it, and that it travels through the very linear thought of it.

For this, I can confidently say that her children's love lives on and travels up to this very moment at the speed of thought to wherever she is.

Chapter Ten

Home

While browsing YouTube, I found a medley by Burt Bacharach and Dionne Warwick doing a duet of the song A House is Not a Home – a Bacharach-David composition. The melody and the lyrics never fail to stir one who seeks perfection. A perfect combination of talent and music could transport one to awe and blissful imagination.

The lyrics can bring one back through time into his childhood – and home, just like Anton Ego in the movie Ratatouille when he was served the dish his mother used to give him as a boy.

A chair is still a chair, even when there's no one sitting there. But a chair is not a house, and a house is not a home when there's no one there to hold you tight and no one there you can kiss goodnight.

True.

My own house sits still on a hill today as it oversees in silence all that has changed over our decades of absence. On the other hand, our ancestral house still stands on the old street where it's been for over half a century. My kids all have great memories with their black Labrador Baxter in the former while I grew up in the latter. Now all faded and parched, my mother's house lay silent on a busy and noisy street. But inside, there is an eerie silence, now empty of children's laughter and piano music. The roof leaks and the floors creak. The kitchen's damp and musty, and the rooms are now cobwebby and dusty.

Although I miss the house, it's not as much as the home. The difference is that a house can only give you cover, but a home is where you feel the vibrations of life. A home is where you hear your babies cry in the night. It is where the sound of kitchenware awakens you. It is where you hear your dad snoring, yet you still get a goodnight's sleep. It is where you hear your dad and mom argue over things because they love you differently. Whatever makes you feel loved, that makes you feel you belong and that makes you become yourself is home – and it could be a person, metaphorically.

We miss people, places, and things not for what they are but because of what we have become with them, when we were in them and when we had them. Whether you were happy or sad in it doesn't matter. What matters is that it has played a role in transforming you into the person you are today simply because you were in it and played your part in the equation.

So, take me home, my Canadian country roads.

Chapter Eleven

Heaven

There's been quite a lot said about Heaven. I am no theologian nor a scholar, so here's an idiot's piece.

The King James version of the Bible mentions the word 327 times in the Old Testament and 255 times in the New Testament, but it appears only 186 times in the New International Version's Old Testament and 236 times in its New Testament. So, where did 160 parts of Heaven go?

Don't panic.

It's right here on Earth, with us.

It's in your home. It's in your workplace. It's on the streets.

It's wherever you find love.

Heaven is where you feel you are loved. It is where you feel everyone is kind and sincere in how they relate to you. Sometimes, it makes me think that Heaven, while we live, is a feeling. So, you have to figure that out – you could already be euphoric and in extreme ecstasy, and yet you're not even anywhere near its gates yet.

Did you notice there's almost no difference between Home and Heaven? It is because heaven is where home is, and home is where you're supposed to feel what heaven is. That's why people say, "he's gone home" when somebody dies – and they're actually referring to heaven.

But, for as long as you're in a place where you feel care and compassion, you're getting a glimpse of heaven.

We're still billions of lightyears away from it, but we're getting there. So, do your little part.

While your feet are on the ground, heaven is all around you. It could be that you're just looking at the wrong things in the wrong places and with the wrong people.

So, go ahead, take a closer look, and get a glimpse of heaven.

Enjoy the sneak preview.

The Camino Chronicles:

Each step through life

is a discovery.

Forward, backward or

no step at all gives

us the lessons.

CHAPTER TWELVE

SOLVITUR AMBULANDO

IT IS SOLVED BY WALKING

FRIEDRICH NIETZSCHE ONCE SAID, *"Truly great thoughts are conceived by walking."*

Most recent studies by Stanford University Graduate School of Education (GSE) professors Daniel Schwartz and Ph.D. Marily Oppezzo have shown that there is a relationship between walking and creativity. Their experiment on 176 students has proven that 60 percent of them were more creative while being tested walking and sauntering on campus versus those who merely sat through the exercise. This experiment was hatched out of the habit of the professors and their students brainstorming while walking.

In 2018, I broached the idea of doing the Camino de Santiago to Maria. Although I have talked to her about it several times before, this time, it was more to find out what her reaction was. Hoping she'd seriously consider it, I went a little further. I said, "Let's do the Camino de Santiago, then let's tour Europe," carefully calculating the words to sound like they were an incentive expecting a positive reaction and answer. Instead, like an unstoppable locomotive train going through a tunnel, my words came out like lightning from one ear to the other.

The trip to Europe became a reality in 2019, but the walk to Camino de Santiago did not. 2020 would have been the year, but Covid 19 closed down the trekking paths to the Camino.

The Camino de Santiago, or the Way of St. James, has always fascinated me, just as millions of others who have trekked towards the church in Santiago de Compostela for over a thousand years. Whatever it was that drew simple folk, royalty, and popes to walk the way held the same compulsion that drew me down that path. Perhaps it is the gnawing desire in our gut to look for answers in life that one can only hope to find, and in this instance - on that road to Santiago. But this is a misnomer. Walking down that road won't give you the answers. The walk within us while walking that road does.

It has been said that after the beheading of St. James in 44 A.D., his body was taken by boat to the Iberian Peninsula, where it capsized amid a heavy storm only to be seen washed ashore covered with scallop shells. Today, the scallop shell has taken on different meanings but mainly as a guide for pilgrims to follow to reach Santiago de Compostela. All over Spain, there are a dozen routes towards it, and all lead to the door of the church at the Plaza do Obradoiro. The popular and traditional route is the 780-kilometer-long French Way which starts at the St-Jean Pied de Port at the foot of the Pyrenees mountains in France. While pilgrims from around the world do the walk for various reasons, the majority do it as a religious devotion to St. James.

We finally did our first Camino in August of 2021, going the traditional French Way but starting in the Galician region. Nine months later, in May of 2022, we did it again, but this time via the Portuguese Way. In both instances, we earned the Compostela, or the certificate of completion written in Latin. We were fortunate to have taken it during the Year of Indulgence as decreed by the Vatican. This means that temporal sins are forgiven plenary if one completes the walk *sine qua non* (an essential condition without which) with confession, forgiving of others, a visit to the tomb of St. James, hearing mass at the cathedral, and receiving of the Holy Eucharist.

After our first Camino, aside from the frameable Compostela, we also brought home the feeling of disbelief that we've finished it at our age. Still, it was only secondary to the overwhelming sense of joy and inner peace we found while doing the walk. Communing with nature has enabled us to see the big picture of life and perhaps drew us closer to who we are. Transformative, they'd always say. But I would rather have that said another way because that has to be seen and felt by others, not us. In the meantime, I'll keep my judgment close to my chest while I continuously walk within myself.

Throughout our walk, we discovered a great deal about who we are as husband and wife and as parents to our children, about who we are as part of the bigger picture of humanity on this blue planet. And about who we are to God and who He is to us.

On the way to the airport coming home, Maria said she couldn't wait to do it again.

Jokingly, I said, "Let's just loop it again from here."

Her look said I was crazy.

Well, she may be right, and maybe I am.

But nine months later, we did the walk again.

Aside from the spiritual part of our first Camino, the introspection was more profound and revealing. I felt like having a great conversation with two friends I have not seen in years. One, a real BFF (Best Friend Forever) – Jesus the Christ; and the other with whom I have developed a love-hate relationship - my favorite frenemy - Me.

While walking, here are some of the things I found out:

That I cannot know myself more based on how others see me and what they prescribe as the conditions under what I must be to fit into their world.

In my scoreboard of life, it is the other way around. *How I see others and their relation to what I can do to make a difference in their lives takes prime consideration.* Seeing it that way enables me to know myself more and how far I can go to achieve that. By nature, there is goodness in all men, but this will only surface by grace when we ask the Lord for it.

We have to ask for it to get it, nothing less.

John 5:30 says, "By myself, I can do nothing. I judge as God tells me."

As we walk through life, we are relentlessly distracted by what people think of us, and we easily fall for it. The social animal in us always wants to please the world. They are made for such a world, and such a world is made for them. The philosopher Georg Wilhelm Friedrich Hegel once said, "To be independent of public opinion is the first formal condition of achieving anything great."

Public opinion, as varied as the number of people in the world, can stop us from becoming what we must become. Well, I'm not surprised that many fall into this trap. Nevertheless, how people portray us should never be our business because we are not in control of it; *what we think of ourselves and what we can do is.* If we let their opinions shape us, then we are trapped in a tight space that will distort our true selves. The only way the opinion of others must matter to us is when they say *we can* - when we think we cannot, and when they say "keep up the good work!" - when we believe we have fallen short of our best. Otherwise, be afraid of four walls. Be claustrophobic of that space!

Go out and be yourself.

Social media has done a great job of defining what is cool and what is not, who fits in and who does not. But let's get real. What is not talked about is that its pages are so full of lonely people craving attention. The "likes" are used to gauge acceptance. The number of views is seen as validation. But do we really need that validation? Aren't we supposed to validate ourselves first? What's the standard? By who's standard?

In this incredible journey through life, true and meaningful "likes" and validation could only come from God. If you don't get that, you have not found yourself yet.

So, the walk on the Camino de Santiago is a great rendezvous trail to meet those two friends I met along the way when we did the walk.

When you do the walk, I assure you –

you'll meet two of the greatest people who walk the face of the earth.

Jesus Christ and Yourself.

On the road to Santiago, we gently

leave the past behind but keep

the lessons learned.

But everything we become

lies waiting at the end of it.

Chapter Thirteen

The Road Within

Men have walked towards their destiny in many ways traveling different roads throughout their lives.

Saul of Tarsus (St. Paul) had the Road to Damascus, Marco Polo did the Silk Road from Italy to China, and Robert Frost did the one less traveled.

For the common part, the symbolic narratives of these journeys have all been captured and well written - Paul's transformation from a vicious soldier to a man of God, Marco Polo's romanticization of his journey leading to the build-up of his influence over the powerful Mongol ruler Kublai Khan and Robert Frost's making a difference by taking the road less traveled.

What I'm saying is that what goes on in our walk on ***The Road Within*** ourselves is the more difficult to pin down. When we can do that, it will be a triumph.

Climbers on Mount Everest do not find the steep craggy edges, the dizzying altitude, and the extreme cold as their worst enemies. They must first climb the Everests lodged in their brains to reach the summit. Sometimes our worst enemies are in our heads, like Trojan horses; they wait for the moment to unleash and slay you. Like a stealthy panther, all they need is a little sign of weakness, then they pounce.

The walk on the Camino de Santiago is no different. It does not throw the most grueling challenges on its road. The most difficult challenge is in us. The distance, the terrain, and the temperature will not make you quit any more than the villains in your head. What can stop you in your tracks is your *will and purpose - or lack thereof.*

The Walk will mean differently to as many as the number of pilgrims there are. Each one holds a unique purpose and motivation. For pilgrims with less spiritual motivations, the rewards may be the tangibles - the prized Compostela, a memorable photograph here, memorabilia there.

But for those searching for a deeper meaning in their lives, the "Road Within" their inner selves presents as much challenge as the Camino Road, where their boots strike the ground.

Like the Camino, the Road Within ourselves is fraught with many challenges and obstacles. The Road Within us holds the heavy boulders of anger, the punishing distance of being unforgiving, the scorching temperature of prejudice, the uphill climbs of woe and regret, and the wayside thorns of hurts and emotional pain. Throughout the Walk, we grapple with demons that threaten to steal away our thoughts and our strength, but then the angels within us fight back and take our steps further one over the other, making each step a blessing. The surprising thing about the Walk is that - there is also the awe of discovering what the human spirit is capable of.

But then, in contrast, like the idyllic landscape of the Galician countryside, it also holds the beauty of compassion for all, the joy of service to others and God, the grandeur of peace and serenity, generosity, gentleness, and the refreshing breeze of love for others.

Walking the Camino Road, one does not only meet the challenges of that long and winding road. It also holds the challenge of discovering your true self - and it is all in this stretch of a "Road Within" yourself. Throughout life, we have met all kinds of people, and we've probably known them more than they know themselves at some point. But knowing ourselves is a more complex task. Too many people die without getting any clear idea of who they are. The great Chinese philosopher Lao Tzu says, "Knowing others is intelligence. Knowing yourself is true wisdom."

The road to Santiago de Compostela is challenging - yes, but the beauty to behold at the end of it will be worth the walk.

In life, all of us walk this road within ourselves. *All our past, we gently leave on this road but keep the lessons learned and everything we can become - wait at the end of it.*

The tricky part is discovering it.

Ultreia et Suseia.

Move higher and further.

CHAPTER FOURTEEN

THE MANY RHYTHMS OF LIFE

I HAD TRAINED HARD for the Camino walk.

Every day I would try to log ten thousand steps straight. On slow days I'd make 8,000 steps so I can safely average 45,000 to 50,000 per week. My mind keeps telling me that I can do it, but it also has the pestering and unpleasant task of convincing my body that it can do it as well. To be effective, it must be relentless, ruthless, and blunt. The 65-year-old body must live up to the strength of the mind and prove it wrong. During my long practice walks, while my mind's already shouting jubilantly *Banzai*! *Banzai*! - my body's still laggardly learning how to do the hand salute. The challenge is to make them fight together against a common enemy, not against each other.

We would strap our backpacks filled with stuff and walk 10 kilometers to find our tolerance in the distance over time and speed. Maria was better prepared as she was logging more than 10,000 steps running between rooms in a massive building at her workplace.

But I needed to be assured that there was harmony between my mind and body. We'd walk from Barondale Drive, south of 401 Highway, all the way down south to the edge of Lakeshore, which is about ten (10) kilometers (6.2 miles) up to midday so that we'd get the hang of it at temperatures mimicking Iberia.

Walking on the Camino de Santiago is a test of your physical capabilities and will - the will to move on despite what the body says, one step at a time. But more than anything else, it is also a test of your character. When I was 13 years old, I'd remember my father attending the *Ultreias* - a monthly meeting of *Cursillistas* (Brothers in Christ who had taken a spiritual retreat called the *Cursilllos* in Christianity) to discuss their brotherhood in service to God and the Church.

When walking the Camino, one is usually greeted either "*Buen Camino*" or "*Ultreia*." For the older generations, they'd say "*Ultreia*," and you are to respond "*et Suseia.*" Now, you're probably wondering what these words mean.

Ultreia is a Calixtine word first heard in the Middle Ages. It means **Move Forward,** and *et Suseia* means **Higher**. Contemplative? Yes. Profound? Yes. But Spiritual? I'd definitely say Yes.

This message, less common today, is of Latin origin and is a word composed of ultra – and eia, an interaction indicating movement. These words are an incitement to continue to the end. The translation would be: "Go further, move forward" – pretty much in the same league as the 1984 Los Angeles Olympics motto Citius, Altius, Fortius (Faster, Higher, Stronger).

Many believe that this greeting would mean that the pilgrims expect to meet again later at the end of their journey - that is, at the door of the Santiago de Compostela church. Yet some also believe that if this was not possible, the wish was to catch up again - higher up, in heaven.

People walk the Camino for different reasons. Some walk to find themselves. Some walk to view their lives backward. Some to find healing and forget a painful past. Some for thanksgiving and others to listen in silence to what God may perhaps have to say to them. Whatever the reasons are, the hope is that they find it at the end of the Walk.

As we began the segment from Palais de Rei to Arzua (28.5 kilometres), we started our steps with our usual praise and worship for the Lord - audibly. We did not care if other pilgrims heard us; they wouldn't understand us anyway. Crazy, they may think of us for doing the audible praises, but come to think of it, walking the Camino has people think pilgrims are crazy. I prayed for mercy and forgiveness, kindness in my heart, patience when I deal with difficult situations, for humility when I tend to focus more on myself.

While I was struggling on the rocky and dusty road, with my prayers between gasps of hurried air, an elderly pilgrim in a motorized scooter rambled through the loosened gravel past me. Whipping up a cloud of dust, he yelled, *"Perdone, ultreia!!"*

I squinted, closed my eyes, and held my breath lest I eat all the dust.

Really?! Doing the Camino in a scooter?!

The nerve.

I felt cheated and disappointed. But I had to trod on, painstakingly slow, just enough to let my weary muscles carry me to the next step.

For all my quick negative thoughts about the Scooter Guy, I asked for forgiveness. Such a quick shift of emotions, wasn't it? Did I not just pray for understanding and patience some kilometres back? I said, Lord, forgive me.

Midway to Arzua, I saw the Scooter Guy again about to get up from his rest atop a grassy mound. As I neared him, I noticed that his body was half-paralyzed and had struggled painstakingly to prep up his scooter.

After a great distance from whence he greeted me, I choked up an answer, and almost like a whisper, I said - "*et Suseia.*"

As he dragged himself awkwardly onto the scooter, I said to myself -

God bless the Scooter Guy.

The person you meet today

won't be the same tomorrow,

just as the person you are

today won't be the same

tomorrow.

Chapter Fifteen

The Rhythm of the Camino

Since starting the Camino, I did not realize right away that Maria and I walked synchronized in our pacing. The rhythm made us forget the punishing steps and motivated us even more to perfect our speed.

Since we began, the only other sounds we'd hear would be our vocalized prayers, the rustling of the leaves in the gusty wind, and the crunching of gravel under our marching shoes and our trekking poles. Both our steps and the clackety crunching of the walking sticks are in perfect rhythm.

For those of you who are music lovers, it's 100 bpm on the metronome scale. To hold up our stamina, we have to have body rhythm. When the noise of the tempo drives us, we forget the daunting distance ahead and our body pains. All we needed aside from the prayers we vocalized was a tempo to get lost into what we were doing - pretty much like a whole Wembley stadium lost in headbanging to the beat of ACDC's You Shook Me All Night Long.

Walking an average of 25 kilometres daily will psych you out (today, we did 22.2 km). When she falls offbeat, I rein in, and she also levels up when I increase my speed. It's a give-and-take situation until we get back into the groove, as it were.

Although we were always mindful of our body and stamina, we couldn't always be sure what was going on in our minds, but the agreed goal was to synchronize our gait as much as possible, given our drive, terrain, and the slope.

In life, it's pretty much the same.

We all take different steps in different directions, never synchronized. (C'mon, we did not even march in precision when we were in the ROTC). When we see somebody not synched with us, we immediately frown and close in on what's wrong with them (not what's wrong with us first!) Then, we put a tag on them – Idiot. Weird. Different. Then we walk away. When they're not up to our speed, we move on and leave them behind like dust after our heels.

We find them strange and square when others don't think and act as we do. We look outwardly and forget to think it could be us who are different.

But really? Do we care to find out what they're going through before we cast the stone?

All of us in this life are not in the same mix of mind, body and spirit at any given time, and we know it. Each one is different from the others. And all of us in this journey goes through changes every day. *The person you meet today won't be the same tomorrow, just as what you are today won't be the You tomorrow.*

We are pilgrims on the Camino of Life and carry different baggage. We carry different hopes and dreams, regrets in life, hurts in our hearts, disappointments, and failures, like our backpacks, some light and some heavy.

So, look again the next time you see somebody different and not in your rhythm.

Be compassionate, be empathetic, be nice, show mercy, show love.

Life is full of turns and blind curves. Somewhere down the road, you'll probably meet the off-beat guy again - but this time, he'll not be the same guy you've judged before.

We all come into other people's lives at different times, and to make judgments or be judged during those times would not be the most fairly deciding moments.

Life's a constant change, and the rhythms we make and follow every day are always syncopated.

So, let's always be kind rather than insist that we're right and that they should "synch" with us.

Who knows, the "different guy who's not in-synch with you today might be the same guy you'll meet down the Camino Road tomorrow.

But this time, you may be the idiot, the weird, the different.

And uh, yes, not at your best.

When we give in to hate,

we cross the boundary

of love's domain.

Chapter Sixteen

Crossing Boundaries

One hundred five years later, on the 17th of May 2022, since the Virgin Mary's first apparition, we were at Fatima, Portugal, to attend its anniversary. With my sister Maria Socorro and her husband Ricardo, we had planned to do the Camino de Santiago in a couple of days, going the Portuguese Way. We had invited our sister Minda Luisa del Carmen to join us, but she was chained to her work.

The Virgin Mary first appeared in Fatima on this day in 1917 and delivered a series of messages to three young children, Lúcia dos Santos and her cousins Francisco and Jacinta Marto. While Mary discussed many things with the children, the messages can be summarized into three invitations:

1. Learn to pray the Rosary. If said daily by families, this simple prayer can change the world.

2. Strive to be spiritually healthy. Penance for our sinfulness and reparations for those we have wronged are the resolutions to achieve that.

3. Keep a devotion to Mary. Let her guide you through life, and you will reach the door of eternity through the gates of Heaven. Once there, you will be happy and forever free from the clutches of mortality. You will live forever.

Since she spoke to children, her messages were simple, direct, and practical - yet they had the profundity of everything so life could be lived according to God's purpose.

I remember our Ateneo grade school activities every October when our Jesuit Headmaster, Fr. Theodore E. Daigler SJ, would let us all converge at the school quadrangle early morning of every Monday of the month to say the Holy Rosary. We'd all pin the blue Marian medals on our school uniform's chests and excitedly gather for a great traditional spectacle – an elocution speech on a piece entitled *Humility Goes Before Glory.* The best grade school orators would stand on elevated wooden platforms to be seen and heard at the far back by the early morning congregation. There was a Grade 7 flat-top kid named Chito Sun in low-waist skinny khaki jeans with a giant Santa Claus buckle whose voice would boom all the way to the back, impressing us Grade 3 pupils. Then there was the handsome and well-mannered kid named Arturo Borja, who's now a Resident Chaplain in a Jesuit boy's school called Xavier. Then we'd do a procession around the Immaculate Concepcion Chapel with the bigger boys carrying the statue of the Virgin Mary. At a time when speaking in our local dialect would cost us a fine of 10 cents, their English diction was a wish to die for.

As I write this, I can recall a few lines of that great piece, thanks to my mother.

"Mary is the greatest woman. She alone outdazzles all others as the sun outshines a meteor. Did she live in luxury? No luxury at the cattle stable where her tiny son slept on a straw." Did she sway a scepter on her throne? Her throne was a weather-beaten cottage in forgotten Nazareth. Was she glorified in this world? No glory as she stood beside her bleeding son on calvary and his enemies, after shaking their fists at the crucified, pointed a finger at her and said – that's his mother!"

So, here we are, right where the greatest woman ever appeared.

May 20, 2022. Lisbon-Fatima-Porto-Braga. All in Portugal.

Even within the country itself, people do not speak the same language in the way they would want to hear and understand. But even if they do, intonations and hand gestures give away different interpretations and separate everyone in different directions. In truly listening with an open heart and mind, can we only see the same vision and catch the same message – but still within the same boundaries. The complexities of human understanding and motivations make it all starkly disuniting.

In life, we cross boundaries within ourselves - and we do that every day.

Daily, we strive hard to become better persons - the version Christ wants us to be, all according to His teachings and the exemplary way He lived His life.

When we give in to hate, we cross the boundary of love's domain. When we speak ill of another person, we cross the boundary of decency and slip a notch down. Inversely, when we give away love, forgiveness and understanding, we cross the boundary of our "old self" and become a "new self," moving a notch higher toward God's grace. We then become better versions of ourselves.

But we discover that it is not easy. The difficulty of it all takes away our focus, forgetting that at the end of the day, it will be our soul's gain many others can just wish for. Many people die along the lonely path, trying hard all their lives to reach the level Christ wants them to achieve. And yet still, many die without even trying. We only fail when we stop trying.

The idea is to try and keep trying while we live. And sadly, many just don't get it.

In a few hours, we shall be crossing the boundary of Portugal and Spain. I am just so bored; I miss my loved ones and friends.

I am about to cross the boundary of myself, bursting with hope as I seek a new me. Buen Camino!

In life, carry only the

bare essentials in

your heart.

Chapter Seventeen

The Baggage of Life

During our 2021 Camino last year, we learned that the lesser things you carry in your backpack, the easier it is to navigate the undulating terrain. The weight of your backpack determines your speed, endurance, and arrival time. The lighter you are, the farther and higher you go. It thus becomes critically necessary to carry only the bare essentials.

But lessons are too often forgotten. More so when 'age' - always the naughty trickster that it is, teases your memory. Already, the baggage of negativity is a heavy cross to bear. Now, add age to that, and you're all stuck in the same muck with nowhere to go.

We left Toronto towards the last part of summer, packed with so many things, forgetting this lesson. Extra shoes, shirts, flashlights, foot gels, Birkenstock sandals, jackets, and a whole pharmacy of kits and pills.

As I grow old, I realize that less is more. Since December 2020, I have tried to eat less and walk more. The more pounds I shed, the better I feel. But that's the physical dimension of my existence. The human spirit is quite different. I believe my soul does not need anything complex but just the 'bare essentials in life.

My friend Lei Bernabe threw in Forgiveness, Love, and Understanding - and I agree!

Forgiveness, so our life becomes light and easy. Hatred is such a heavy stone for the soul to carry.

And Love, yes.

Love - to share with everyone regardless of color and belief. A love shared is an exponential multiplier that returns a hundredfold.

And, Understanding!

So those with shorter reach can catch their dreams while they stand on your shoulders.

I want to add a few essentials, though. Let me add Family, Friends, and Prayers. And you may add your own too.

At the end of each day, don't we all wish we see and feel our Family in the warmth and comfort of our home? At life's end, many a deathbed only saw a family member gently sit by the passing loved one.

At the end of each day, don't we all wish we did something good for Friends and others? One good deed for a friend might be that he had hoped for all his life.

At the end of each day, don't we wish our Prayers were granted? A particular prayer might be the one the Lord was waiting for you to say to show you how powerful and glorious He is.

So, my friend, the baggage on your back spells your luck as your boots hit the ground.

But the baggage of your soul spells your grace, or the lack of it, as you move towards your real Home.

So, try this: *Carry only the bare essentials.*

Walking the Camino isn't much

about becoming anything.

Maybe it is about unbecoming

everything that is not

really you.

Chapter Eighteen

This is the Day the Lord has Made

Let us be glad and rejoice in it

AUGUST 23RD, 2021.

Today, we walk from A Rua to Santiago de Compostela and end the last leg of the Camino.

It is some 22 kilometers through hills, cornfields, and grazing land. Since the Pilgrim's mass is at noon, we must leave at 6:00 am.

My wake-up alarm went off at 5:30. I checked the temperature. 17C (62.6F). Great! We packed everything we needed the night before - maps, credentials, Camelback bladders, foot Vaseline, windbreakers - all neatly jammed into my 35L backpack. Heavy? Yes, about 18 pounds. Maria had about 10.

For all the reasons I have yet to know, I believe a lot of people walking the Camino carry more than the weight of their belongings. What do I mean by this?

Somebody said that when walking the Camino, you leave behind all that you are on the road and become what you will be at the end in Santiago.

When we started our first morning, we came upon a forked road to the Camino. We stood there momentarily, waiting for somebody to point us the right way. Both ways had the Camino scallop arrow sign. Suddenly, a green wooden window shutter swung open, and an old lady told us, "*Ese es el viejo, así es más corto y más bonito,*" pointing to the road on the right. I told Maria the lady was saying this way is shorter, and the view is beautiful. Then the lady said, "Buen Camino!"

That was our first blessing from anyone ever on this walk. This hit me immediately, and I kept thinking about it for several kilometers.

In life, we must always speak our blessing.

From the time they were as young as 8, all my children would give us the priestly blessing every time Maria and I would leave the house.

The Lord bless you and keep you,

The Lord make His face shine upon you and be gracious to you

The Lord lift up His countenance upon you and give you peace

(Numbers 6:22-27)

They'd even shout it out from their bed, half asleep, when they'd hear us heading out the door. We consider this a basic family tradition, which has become a ritual over the years. We bless each other for everything that we do and wherever we go.

When we speak our blessing to others, it unleashes God's favor to whom we give it. The blessing puts them under God's protection and puts wind in their wings so they can move toward the Lord's direction. For us who give it away, the spoken blessing creates a hollow in our hearts for God's mercy and grace to replenish and fill in. The more we give the blessing, the bigger the room for grace and mercy.

Throughout our Camino walk, the blessings of "Buen Camino" from everyone have filled our souls with energy and gladness, leaving no room for anything not of God. The words gave wings to our feet, empowering our steps forward. Peregrinos walking the Camino would freely say it to you when they pass you, and we do the same.

When we say, "God bless you" to another, it comes back to us many times. When we receive a blessing from someone, we level up in goodness. When I get a "Buen Camino," I feel empowered to move on. When we give it back, we shred everything negative and heavy, leaving us lighter and more agile. We then become less of who we are and become more of Him. When we give away the blessing, we lift our souls higher.

Someone said that walking the Camino isn't much about becoming anything. Maybe it is about un-becoming everything that was not you and becoming the You that was meant to be in the first place.

Well, both ways, I say yes. Un-become the lesser You so that you can become the more of Him.

Irish playwright George Bernard Shaw once said, "Life isn't about finding yourself. It is about creating yourself."

I disagree a bit with the semantics, and I say you cannot create anything out of nothing unless you are God. You have to find yourself first and then re-create yourself.

If you are still trying to find yourself now, I cannot offer you an answer, much less give you all the answers you've been seeking all your life.

But for any reason, you might one day do the Camino walk; your answer may perhaps lie at the end of the road.

Just as you're about to quit,

the Lord chuckles at your folly!

Don't give up!

Chapter Nineteen

Keep the Faith

The walk from Sarria to **Portomarin** is a good 24.4 kilometers. We left at 8:40 am in a nippy 12c and arrived at 5:05 pm, walking thru small villages and pastures. The terrain was rocky and dusty with uphill slants of about 20-grade. But the view at the top of Pena do Corvo in A Coruña was breathtaking, and so were the tiny hamlets and tree-lined paths along the way.

As we were nearing Portomarín (and nearly passed out from total exhaustion), and as if the punishing distance and terrain were not enough, the path became even more steep downhill with loose stones and boulders as big as a Volkswagen Beetle along a narrow opening walled by wild vegetation and mossy fences.

Finally reaching the edge of a long steel bridge towards Portomarin, and just as our knees were about to give up! - staring at us with that menacing look - the iconic stairway to the town's gate all steep and long. Even before I started the first step, my knees trembled every time I glanced at the steps.

I did not want to think of anything other than just the steps I had to take each carefully. All the way up, I just looked down at my feet. When we reached the top, the anxiety of looking for our hotel Albergue would have delivered the coup de grace.

But the Lord knew it all along, and what sense of humor He has. I could almost see His face snicker at the wings of the stage. Twenty steps (!) ahead, izquierda was our albergue.

Perfect timing. Great reward.

So it is with life, my friends.

Just when you are about to give up, the Lord chuckles at your folly.

He's already figured out your reward all along.

Keep the faith!

One day, what love you gave

to your children will come back

to you in your most unexpected

and unguarded moments.

Chapter Twenty

The Circle of Life

On a long and lonely countryside path today between Pontevedra and Caldas de Rei in northern Spain, we walked behind a couple with the dad carrying his son on his back. He must have been carrying about 45 pounds, given he had other things on him. It was a searing 27c, like a noonday heat in my native country.

But he was brisk and happy.

This scene took me back to a night in 1960 when I was about four years old. My parents took me to a movie theatre in my native Cagayan de Oro called Lyric along Calle del Mar Street. We've watched the last full show of Ben-Hur, a Charlton Heston classic. It is a great movie but meaning no irreverence to it, I slept. I slumped on my wooden seat about half of it (because I don't remember the full screenplay), and my father carried me in his arms as he and mom walked home.

I still vividly remember being half awake on the way (in front of what is now Universal Hardware along Gomez St.), but nonetheless, he still carried me about two blocks away until we reached home. This scene keeps coming back to my mind over the years whenever I think of him.

I have seen a lot of pictures on Facebook and in magazines about sons carrying their debilitated fathers in situations many other children wished they had the opportunity to do and pay back.

I was not given this opportunity.

My father died at 3:15 am in my mother's arms as he succumbed to a heart attack in 1986. I was then living separately with my young wife and son Popoy.

In life, there are situations where great moments are created between parents and children. Be on the lookout for these. One day, what love you gave to your children, comes back to you in your most unguarded and vulnerable moments. You'll know it when it happens because it will create a spark in your memory, just as this scene did today.

Only then will you realize that you have gently closed the circle...

the circle of life.

Life is still a friend, even if

you think it is a stranger

who doesn't deserve you.

Chapter Twenty-One

Life Plays Harvey Dent

Life is a friend wearing a stranger's mask. When you get what you want out of it, friend, it is. But otherwise, it is a stranger.

Harvey Dent was simply a good citizen of Gotham until life betrayed him. Splashed with acid on one side of his face, he became bitter. He became the Two-Faced Criminal. Life may sometimes not give you a kind and fair hand, but the rule to keep is to remain fair – even if others are not, will not, and cannot. It is not winning that truly matters in life but playing fair.

When you get a raise in pay, life is a friend, and you say – aah, life thou art fairest of all! - even if you think you don't deserve a penny. When you discover that love follows you everywhere, you smile and tell yourself – This is life! Or when you bask out in the sun on a breezy afternoon with an ice-cold beer in your hand – you close your eyes, burp, and mumble to yourself - life is good! Well, I'm not going to argue with you, so yes, life is a friend.

Life only becomes a stranger when we don't get what we want and don't understand why we are in a fix we disagree with. When we don't understand why life is unfair, it becomes as strange as a geometrical formula we are unprepared to understand. It becomes a stranger when we get the shorter end of the stick, and we see ourselves standing alone under a streetlamp on a foggy and damp night with nowhere to go. It becomes a stranger when we wrestle with questions of why we are left out, rejected in the cold, holding an empty cup, getting no answers – and friends are simply nowhere to be seen.

But either way, the good thing is, pinch yourself now - you are alive.

I have friends who have become strangers. Friends I've known since kindergarten. Friends since the days when life was as simple as pushing a marble down a tiny hole. But over the years, the complexities of life have scattered the marbles all over. While some friends have taken the oft-beaten paths, others have created their own and given up on friendships. Some have gone beyond a far distance, never to show their faces again, while some remained in their old corner only to die with a flower or two on their graves. Life, indeed, takes us away in all directions.

As years go by, there are people who are unable to keep up with the speed of change. They begin to yearn for the life they've lost, hoping to fill a void with the things of yesterday. Whatever it is, they'd clutch it like they were drowning in a whirlpool of emptiness. That's why they always return to familiar places hoping to find the same friends at the usual places – the park bench, the old café hoping to catch the familiar feeling again. They'd visit the old bar, put a coin in the old jukebox, and play their old songs - only to find out that no one was there left to dig their kind of music.

But the saddest thing I've discovered is that there are friends who have simply shut themselves off from the world. While we may find it strange and feel sorry for them, we may never know the reality. Because the truth is, they may be the happiest freakin' hermits in the world celebrating their solitude, ecstatically thankful they don't see your face anymore. And that is why they simply shut everyone off. So, always shoot down your expectations. Zero expectations never hurt.

And today, there are strangers who I have become friends with. Heraclitus once said, "Everything changes but Change itself. Everything flows, and nothing stays the same." The truism, therefore, that "there is no permanent thing in this world than change itself" is true. If everything had stayed exactly the same, we wouldn't be where we are today – we'd still be writing our history with firewood ash through our drawings on cave walls.

When I was eight, my dad gave me a set of toy soldiers, about 8 inches in height each. In that set, my favorites were the grenade thrower, the sniper, and the commander. They were my fiercest arsenal of friends. I'd position them hidden behind rocks and order them to battle when the enemy slackened. I'd throw stones at the enemy, and when they'd topple, I'd regroup my squad for the victory parade.

I stopped playing with them when I got older as they no longer appealed to me. I stashed them back to their barracks in boxes under my bed, completely lost and forgotten – only to find out my mother gave them away to some friend's child. Slum books, 45 rpm records of Sam the Sham and the Pharaohs, The Beatles, Woodstock '69, and the guitar became my new friends.

Now, here's my point: As we move forward in life, there are things we leave behind as we look forward to new things that give meaning to us – things that will make more difference in our life.

When we came to Canada, we left behind everything that mattered: Family, jobs, friends, and everything that we love. Strangely, it was like coming into a new home with an empty cupboard; we had to stock up on things to survive. While some friends still keep in touch to this day, others have not. While we struggled as newcomers in a strange country, some friends made our transition easy as they stood by us every step of the way. Others were simply not seen even from a far distance – but that will be a whole new book to write about. There will always be gaps in any relationship, and as time moves on, some gaps close while some become unconnectable. These ones sometimes keep us stranded on a spot making us unable to move forward. We have to force the bitter reality under our skin that God does not give us the people we *want* to be around; He gives us the people that we *need* to make us become who we are. Just like my toy soldiers when I positioned them to get a good advantage, God positions the people around us to give us the greatest strategic advantage – even if we may not like some of them.

At some point, you meet people along the path of life to make or unmake you, pushing out open your authentic self. They are part of your metamorphosis. They will change your life forever just as you will change theirs. Some will stay for years until they have completed their assigned task of molding you. They could be your parents, teachers, friends, and family.

Some will stay for your lifetime – perhaps your spouse, children, or friends.

Others may appear in your life like a flash, but all of them have a place in your life to shape you into what you ultimately become. There is always a reason for their specific roles in your timeline.

How you interact with them will be your share in unmasking your true and real self. Whether they will be a blessing or a thorn in your side depends on how you react.

Friend or foe - always your call.

And that's life.

So, pinch yourself again this time and wake up to this reality -

Life still wants you to be a friend, even if you think it is a stranger you don't deserve.

While some may already have

found life to be good, others

are still searching for the

good in life.

Chapter Twenty-Two

I Read the News Today, oh Boy!

I recently read the news in our high school group chat that Donny Osmond had died.

To us, he will always be known as Donny Osmond. When a classmate at Xavier would say, "I just saw Donny Osmond at the grocery store," we'd right away know who he's referred to or when they'd say in class, "uh-oh, Donny Osmond just got into trouble with the Physics professor," we'd all turn our eyes on him.

And "him" is my good friend, Jonathan.

He had the maxillary semblance of that Donny Osmond toothy grin hence the moniker. He did not once protest or discourage it, but his blush was the tacit answer that he loved the tag. In the 70s, the real Donny Osmond was such a heartthrob that girls would gladly trade their dad's Cadillac Fleetwood for, and the moniker may have worked in Jonathan's favor. Besides, to go against a bullying mob of rowdy lunatics lumped into one class was just plain Kamikaze dive. If indeed it was bullying, it was bullying that made the victim feel good.

I first knew Jonathan when I was in Grade 7. Once in high school, we had a sleepover at a beach house with a group of classmates invited to join a "teach-in" by a cadre of Maoists. Except for one or two in that group, the rest were just there to enjoy the pebbled beach and the music. Our young minds were too crowded with girls even to leave a tiny space for Chairman Mao. Jonathan was a good guitar player, and I was amazed at how he deftly fingered the chords. I only knew the basic D major, A minor, and G major, but he knew a lot more that I bugged him no end to teach me The Monkees' I Wanna Be Free. And that, my friends, was the first full-length song I learned on my guitar.

He had transferred to Xavier Ateneo all-boys Grade School from Manila. Together with some children, he and his brother Ben were sponsored by American Peace Corps volunteers to study at the Malate Elementary School but had to go back to their province of origin when the tour of duty of the volunteers had ended.

When we graduated from high school, I saw less of him except once when he played the clarinet for the university marching band. Band members earned free tuition, which was how he fared through college. Coming from a large and crowded family, I could imagine the need to keep moving all over just to keep the balance, and for this, he also had to work part-time as a student assistant at the admissions testing center to cover his other needs.

Even after I'd finished my economics degree and moved on further to law school, he was still halfway through college, as I would later come to know. The next thing I knew, he had married a farm girl and had six kids.

While the rest of us began to transcend from Need to Want, he was still in the Need stage. While the rest of us were already out dating girls at night, he was still out late doing work overtime. While we had begun the good life, he was still searching for the good in it - and I know what this means - my mom had eleven other siblings.

Suddenly, life was a bitter-sweet juggle of raising small children, playing for the band, and working late evenings at the university campus. Once in a while, when old classmates would gather, I'd see him sing his heart out, drowning all the conversations with his ultra falsetto version of Stevie Wonder's All in Love is Fair. But listening to him yelp his lungs out made me suspect that it was more to drown out all his sorrows.

I have twice pulled him up into jobs that may have re-directed his life. First into the bank where I worked after college, and then into another finance company whose president was a friend of mine. He lost both jobs. The Asian Financial Crisis retrenched him in the first one, and he resigned from the latter for a supposedly better one – unfortunately, he left that one too.

As the years passed, we seldom had the chance to meet up for coffee except for a couple of times when we got together for a friend's birthday. Both occasions were successful Beatles comeback concerts. As long as Donny

Osmond was there with his guitar and a repertoire of Beatles songs, the night should be good.

All is fair in love, he sang - indeed, it may have been fair to him as he loved his wife and kids so much, and they loved him back, but for those double-whammy job losses, life itself may not have been kinder.

I remember one night when he ran out of songs; our conversations turned serious and morbid. Between rounds of gin and tonic, the topic turned to dying, legacies, and epitaphs. "What would you like to be written on your epitaph?" they asked each.

Booze and melancholia are a miserable mix, as I found it strange even to join that conversation. As they silently waited for my answer, I said, *"One day, you'll find to see I'm gone, but tomorrow may rain, and so I'll follow the sun."* It was a line from the last song we sang before we opened another bottle of Ginebra San Miguel Quatro Cantos.

I was not quite sure what he said for his part, except that he mumbled through a loud burp so gross it reeked so much alcohol you could turn his breath into a flamethrower with a single spark.

The last time I saw him was before I left for Canada. He had confided that a daughter had wanted to go abroad to work and that, hopefully, he could finally take a bow and retire. After a few drinks, like wolves howling at the moon, we began another Beatles concert. I remember him singing Norwegian Wood with an encore.

A few years ago, he died of a massive heart attack, leaving a family unprepared. When they posted pictures of his tombstone on Facebook, I was taken aback when I saw the words written on the marble epitaph: *"One day, you'll find to see I'm gone, but tomorrow may rain, and so, I'll follow the sun."* Thanks, Donny Osmond, for that great preclusion!

English Philosopher Francis Bacon said, "A man dies as often as he loses his friends." Jonathan was one of the few friends that I had. I felt myself die a little when I read the news. Oh boy.

A few days ago, I saw his wife Aurora on Facebook enjoying autumn in Norway after attending a daughter's wedding there. My wife Maria had phoned her a few months back saying I could be there if they needed somebody to give away the bride, and I would have gladly done it, but I guess they wanted it to be private. If Jonathan were alive today, he would have sung Norwegian Wood right in the heart of Norway.

Sometimes life does not hand you the fruits of what you dream and work for, no matter what. But hey, sometimes it does - without even going up on stage *yourself* to claim the prize. You could swear to eat fire or sword many times over to get what you want, but if it's not meant to be, nothing can change that. Not everything happens like in the movies where heroes always win and ride into the sunset.

Well, except for one movie, though -

In the movie Braveheart, Mel Gibson, as Sir William Wallace, after being hanged, drawn by a horse, and quartered, dies by beheading without seeing the ultimate victory of the Scottish Longshanks at Bannockburn. Although he was not at the victory ball, his smile rode into the sunset.

Jonathan had his eyes set so hard on his children's dreams he may have passed by himself along the way, and going too fast, he might have pretended there was no end so that they'd all reach their dreams - even when he already had his first stroke and was half-paralyzed. But for Jonathan, I knew that everything he did was something bigger than himself. I've always known him to be selfless, and everything he strove for doesn't just add up except to point to the reality that it was for others but himself. I've known people who work their backs off not to get what they want but to have their children get what they want - and they're fully conscious of this every moment of their working life. And indeed, when it's over, and the children all succeed, the joy of fulfillment is even sweeter – and that would have been Jonathan's case except that we won't see that smile on his face anymore.

Life doesn't always end the way people envision it. While we all pray to see our dreams come true before we die, there is no guarantee. But let me tell you this: Hard work and prayer will always give it to you, maybe not in your lifetime but to those you've sacrificed for. Sometimes God puts it that way to make your descendants realize how much you've worked hard for them in case they didn't notice the first time. And when they finally do, they'll appreciate your love even more than they've ever done.

Today his lovely wife Aurora and the girls are in Norway, starting their own life there. It would have been nice if Jonathan had been there with them. It is almost autumn as I write this, and the leaves will soon fall. The canopy of those fallen leaves would quickly cover all his hard work, broken dreams, and sacrifices.

But like Braveheart Wallace, bound face-up on the executioner's table at the town square - just before the axe fell, gave his last look at the love of his life Murron McClannough from the corner of his eyes... and smiled.

It was a smile that spoke of victory.

Right now, Jonathan may be smiling as he looks at his beloved family from the corner of his eyes.

And so, I say the view from where I sit is no better than where Jonathan is.

Above the clouds, with a guitar in his hand, I could almost hear him sing, "Isn't it good, Norwegian Wood."

Happy things

live forever.

CHAPTER TWENTY-THREE

LIFE IS A JIGSAW PUZZLE

WE'RE ALL PIECES OF EACH OTHER'S PICTURE PUZZLES

We all wonder where souls go when the body dies.

I say it all depends on what we believe in. Hindus believe the soul reincarnates and take on other life forms. Buddhists believe that souls are reborn infinitely until they settle in Nirvana. Christians believe in salvation and the life hereafter that even as grown-ups, they still keep the idea that angels carry the soul to heaven.

But what about the living? What happens to those who are left behind when their loved ones die?

Twenty years after my father died, my mother never regained her everyday life back. She would sag on her couch and watch television the whole day until she fell asleep. We would literally raise her deadweight with our baseball dug-out words to rise and go out onto the sun, but she would remain stuck in her miserable spot with nowhere to go.

Life seemed to have left her long before she died in 2013. She died with a heart wrapped in grief and loneliness. I tell you, souls die a thousand times long before the body does.

Writer Jamie Anderson once said, *"Grief, I've learned, is really just love. It's all the love you want to give but cannot. All of that unspent love gathers in the corners of your eyes, the lump in your throat, and in the hollow part of your chest. Grief is just love with no place to go."*

Life is like a thousand-piece jigsaw puzzle.

You'll never see the complete picture until each piece settles in its place. Once a piece is lost, the picture can never be whole again. Each piece has a specific spot that cannot be filled by just any other. Friends and strangers come in different forms and sizes and will have specific spots in your life's jigsaw puzzle. But it is different when a loved one dies because their death disintegrates the whole puzzle. You may not want to put all the pieces together again this time.

Our friend Jay lost his wife Agnes to cervical cancer a couple of years ago after a long and painful struggle. Like Siamese twins, they were inseparable. She was a talented artist, and just like her art, their union was like a prized masterpiece. Jay is the frame, so he goes where the art is. One is never complete without the other, as it were. He's one of the most supportive husbands I know - complementing Agnes in quiet strength all through their 35 years of marriage in whatever dynamics of a fix they'd find themselves in. In silent pride, he would imperceptibly bask in his little sphere of joy at the back of the room where he'd always prefer to be, watching her do her art and room decorations. But his beam of ebullience would easily give him away when we'd compliment the brilliance of Agnes' works. Becoming discernible when this happens, we know right away that he loves her so much. Whatever makes her happy - makes him happy. Life's simple pleasures, if I were to borrow that worn-out cliché. But such is the pleasant irony in life that you lose something in yourself when you chip out a part of you, yet never feel more whole than when you give it away.

Indeed, when one gives, one receives multiplied.

Their relationship was this way in more ways than one can imagine. Agnes was a noted architect back home in her native country. Her attention to detail in art and design was uncompromising, yet her finished works would always turn out to be classically impressive. Every time her artistic streak would break loose, even a dull and lifeless room would spring to life when she'd put her touch on it. She was a Midas, but he was the silent pillar in her court.

By divine design, Jay rode with us in the car not too long ago. We had just concluded a great weekend at a beach cottage some two-and-a-half hours drive away from home with a small group of friends. It was a chop-suey mix of the sad, the glad, and the lonely - all accomplished by some measure and all bound by this sheer faith in the Master Artist of all. Great couples who would otherwise still have their stubborn shadows to tame, myself included.

Jay was sequestered from his condominium by his old friends from back home, Bob and Pauline – a great couple who's perfected the art of friendship; I thought they were best friends when I first met them. Naturally altruistic and caring, they'd always check on him, concerned about how he coped. Always looking for the right moment to rescue him, that Friday was the perfect day. Jay was unsuspecting of the Why, the What and the Where To of his sequestration when they picked him up that afternoon for the long drive. Knowing the guy, for as long as his six-pack Coors Light in his ubiquitous handy Igloo box was with him, he'd always go and be a willing kidnap victim ready to embrace Stockholm Syndrome. Since Bob and Pauline's house would come first on the way home, we invited Jay to ride with us since his condo unit is just two blocks from where we live.

The drive back was technically tricky. It was past eight in the evening, and it was raining. Worsening the situation was the narrow merging of lanes by road construction and the damn-if-you-do-damn-if-you-don't speed of 120kph (75mph), which you must maneuver to keep pace with the thousand other speedfreaks going over the speed limit. Given all these, I could only do a feeble "yes, that's right, uh-huh" and a gentle nod over the rear-view mirror to an otherwise great exchange of thoughts between my wife Maria and Jay about the loss of such a great lady in Agnes. Maria said that while it was sad she could not see Agnes during her last days, it was also a pleasant comfort to perpetually retain a beautiful image of her, so radiant and full of life. Maria told him how hesitant we were in reaching out to him after she passed, unsure if he'd see callers and well-wishers, preferring instead to heal first until he's ready to walk out again into the real world. We knew he'd all be recoiled into his solitary period of mourning.

And yes, it turned out we were right.

He had bubbled himself deep into his world of recovery, inching his way back piece by piece, step by step, just like a jigsaw puzzle. He'd grown his hair and beard long and did not call and return calls from concerned friends. His children, all grown up, wanting him to move on, gave him two sets of a hundred-piece jigsaw puzzle. He'd spend days trying to piece together the puzzles (and of his whole puzzle of life literally) up to the limits of where his Coors light and his sanity would take him.

Lonely hearts never travel far. They tend to endlessly drag their feet around in circles picking up the pieces of their broken dreams. So, he'd while his time on the jigsaw puzzles hoping to claw his way up from the rubbles. And this was what his children wanted to happen - keep him busy, so he'll not dwell on the pain.

In the car, Jay had confided that he was never prepared to lose Agnes, even up to the last moment when he touched her lifeless face at 1:00 am during her sleep. He had rubbed his nose gently on her sweet, emaciated face to find out if she was still breathing. Jay had told God how he and Agnes served Him and that He should not allow all this pain to happen to her. Up to the last minute, he said he had expected a miracle, never expecting anything less. That's why he was never prepared to see her go.

But no miracle happened.

His life came spiraling down into disbelief and denial when she finally breathed out the final stroke of her brush. So yes, Jay stared endlessly at the jigsaw puzzles through his sleepless nights. The pieces never fell into place easily, but it certainly made his days easier.

Maria said that if Agnes were alive, she would certainly not want to see Jay in the direction he's moving his life without her. She would have wanted him to celebrate her memory by going out with friends, traveling the world, and putting on a happy and brave face towards the remaining years of his life. Maria believed that with this demeanor, he would give a great lesson of survival for others to learn when they, too, lose a loved one.

Agnes loved him for what he was; he should not lose himself by un-becoming the person she loved.

Maria had said that Agnes' purpose in life had been served according to the Lord's plan, and it had been accomplished. This consolation alone should hasten his healing so he can move forward.

Jay had said he was moving out of his condo unit soon and live with one of his children. He said he discovered that among the things Agnes cherished was a child's painting. It was a painting my granddaughter Maia gave her on her birthday, showing two matchstick people in love and holding hands together with little hearts raining all over. The inscription says, "To Tita Agnes, Love from Maia." Every time we visited Agnes at her condo back when she was alive, she'd show us this miniature painting, always forgetting she'd already shown it to us a thousand times before and saying over and over again how she loved it and loved Maia then always end by saying the painting never fails to put a smile on her face.

I broke my silence.

While my eyes were still carefully glued to the road, my heart wanted to join the conversation. I said, "When you move out and sort everything in your home, carefully go over Agnes' stuff; do not take everything with you. Leave behind those that will carry the pain of losing her. But be sure to bring those that put a smile on Agnes' face. You would know those things. Whatever made her smile, take them with you. These will carry you through when the road ahead gets tough."

All the friends that came together during that weekend were there for very specific roles. Their place in Jay's life was pre-destined and pre-designed like pieces of the jigsaw puzzle. As the weekend unfolded, each one stepped into their place in the puzzle to make Jay's life partially complete.

When a loved one dies, we see life shatter into a thousand pieces. And they all say you must pick up all the pieces one by one to repaint the happy picture and move on.

But I'd say it differently for Jay. I say you do not pick up everything. Leave behind the sharp shards that will keep on wounding you. Pick only the ones that will put a smile back on your face. By doing that, you're also putting a smile on the face of the loved one gone. All the broken pieces will never give you the same old picture as before, so only pick the ones that will give you a happy picture.

Because happy things live forever.

When we got home, I checked the backseat to see if Jay had left anything. He had left an unopened Coors Light on his armrest.

As we entered the house, I gently patted Maria's back. "You've just made a weary soul happier tonight. You've matured so much; I admire your eloquence". I told her as I gently closed the door behind us.

Roller coasters give you the

best view from the top,

but the sudden drops and

lowest points give you

the best lessons.

Chapter Twenty-Four

Life is from Point A to Point B

I was in my office on the 21st floor of a building along Ayala Avenue in Makati, the Philippines' business district. Every day I would see people below walking like ants from the colossal glass window behind me. They were the usual people that would go about where they were supposed to go at a particular time of day, just as I'd watch them a thousand times. It seemed like it was a routine so hard to break. People are antsy, frantically crawling from Point A to Point B daily.

I checked my watch - 5:30! It was going to be my last day in office as I just formally did my early retirement.

As I was gathering my things, my direct superior, who was Chief Operating Officer, came up to me for the last time and asked, "So Bob, is this final? Are you really sure you're leaving us?" I said, "Yes, ready to go!" giving him a quick glance. I was firm, but I guess my voice gave me away as there was a bit of sadness in how I said it. And he goes - "You're messing up our succession plans." In one of our branch visits a year before, he had asked me if I was ready to be Executive VP. I had nothing to say about that and didn't - even if I had. I still had to go home and pick up the wife and the kids. Headstrong in my rush to leave early, I could only give him a wry smile.

Four hours later, my family and I were at the Ninoy Aquino International Airport for our flight to Canada.

My entire working life has only been just me and my career. So, no family and not even God. Nothing else came close. It seemed like I was killing myself for the glory of my career, period. Sadly, we don't realize that until a curve ball hits us.

On several occasions, I would forget a son's birthday; once, I even forgot it was our wedding anniversary.

My friends back home had a word for it – Success.

Career success? Perhaps, but is that the be-all-end-all? What about work and family balance? What they didn't know was that there was a heavy price that I paid for it. Bill Gates once said that Success is a lousy teacher, and I think he's right.

It's always the failures and defeats that give us the greatest lessons. So, if I were to create my definition, I would not call failures – failures; and defeats - defeats. They are not the end of it all. I'd call them teachers – because failures and defeats taught me the greatest life lessons. And Confucius bears this one out. He once said, "*there are a thousand lessons learned in defeat but only one in victory."* He's right about the thousand and one lessons in defeat because it takes that many to perfect a victory.

The price I had to pay was that since I had been a slave to my career, I was always away from my family, and that, to a great degree, was a failure. So many things happen when people are away from their loved ones; let me say that with all the perks, they could become jerks.

We arrived on July 1, Canada Day.

For me, it was a blessing because, finally, all of us would be *together in one place* after being away for long periods - and many years. I have been assigned all over the place in the Philippine archipelago overseeing a network of branches engaged in finance and lease. Soon after we arrived, our two older boys and Maria found jobs. They were starter jobs, but they were okay with it.

However, I could not find work despite being confident in my qualifications. As the months passed with so many job applications unanswered, I became depressed and bored. I'd stay in bed for most of the day.

While I was wasting away, Maria had to put on a brave face despite feeling so tired after coming home from work lest she'd infect the children with all the viral frustrations slowly wearing us out. Had she flinched, she would have felt responsible if we all broke apart, she later confided.

It was the Freddie Mac and Fannie May recession when we first arrived, and thousands were out of work. Although Canada was a border away to the north with distinct economic policies and a robust economy latched on healthy indexes, she was slumped face down.

It was only the following year that I finally found a job, and it was not even within my field of experience. While there was a lot of pain in not finding work, seeing my family struggle was the greater pain.

And yet, God knew what I was going through because I prayed so hard for it. He was just not giving me the answer.

As the days went by, I began to question Him in silence.

Half of me kept the bravado intact, saying I should believe in myself, and yet half would say, "keep on praying." So, there was like a tug-of-war going on inside me. I was shifting between trusting God and doubting Him.

But the sad thing was that every time I kept Him out of my mind, depression would creep in. As the days turned into weeks and months into a year, I realized I was missing the point - because, for the longest time I thought God was not answering my prayers; I realized He wanted me to do something rather than just idly wait.

Here's what I found out: *For all my years of absence from family life, God wanted me to make up and know my family more genuinely.*

When we arrived, we were cramped in a tiny two-bedroom apartment where all the boys would be in one room and Maria and I in the other. On our first night, we slept on cardboard we had spread over the wooden floor after we unpacked our things. We looked at one another in silence and asked ourselves if we had made the right decision. It was something we did not imagine beyond all the excitement. Over the next several days, Canadian friends from back home delivered used beds, a dining table, a television (!), and a rundown sofa which must have seen quite a lot of drama over many generations aside from a bonus of M&Ms in between its cracks. What made the adjustments even harder was the temperature change.

And we just did all things together. We ate together, hungered together. We huddled together during the coldest days. And for whatever little we had, we just laughed away our troubles – pretty much the surest way I felt best to settle in, even with all our burden.

But we did something we've not done in a long time. At the end of the day, we'd gather around the dinner table and pray together. So, little by little, God showed me what I missed about being a *present* father and a husband.

But I did not get this right away. There was so much pride in myself, believing that I could still do things the old way, and this made my little world warped so that I could not get the Lord's message. It was only when I shredded off all pride and told myself clear that I was nothing without my God and that all grace could only come from Him that I began to have inner peace. I would start my day with thanksgiving and offering everything that may come.

Humility is the clear lens that makes us see things God wants us to see. Without it, life would be a blur, and we won't have clarity of purpose.

God has put you today where you should be. You are not where you are to fill a space. You are the leading actor in your life. You are not just a supporting background character walking behind somebody else's central part. Life would not be the same without you, just as other people's lives won't be the same without you in there. The places you've been to and the people you've interacted with have evolved because of your presence. Somehow, the little things you may have done along the way have made a difference in the lives of others, and that's for sure.

So, stop flying around thinking you should be somewhere. Touch down on the spot you are sitting while reading this because that is your place at the present time and space. Acts 17 says, "God decides the exact time of your birth and the exact place where you should live." So, not a second too soon and not a second too late in your time of birth. And not an inch more or less of where you're supposed to live. Everything is exact.

My nursery records say I was born at 1:06 in the morning of February 22nd, and my home address now is triple 5-3 Toronto, Canada – which is my exact space at this very time.

God is in absolute control of time and space up to a millionth of the speed you blink your eye. Everything is exact and pre-destined. So, for us, it was never a coincidence – because everything that happened to us happened according to His timetable.

I want to share with you three lessons I have learned about why God has planted us here.

The first lesson is - that time with family trumps everything. If you have your family with you at arm's length today, you're already a lottery winner! When you're all together, it does not matter if you argue and bicker; that's okay - love will not go away. *Your worst days together as a family will still be better than your best times with others.* Love will always endure.

Secondly, for all the times I thought God was not answering my prayers, I realized He wanted me to build my faith first. So, the next time you ask something from Him and don't get what you want, *find out what He wants you to do first.* And what you do during waiting tests your character and faith.

Sometimes His blessings are not in the things He gives you, but in those He withholds from you. Barbara Morgan, a second-grade teacher from Idaho, was the alternate astronaut to join the space shuttle Challenger. She had vied along with 11,000 other teachers to be selected for the Challenger space program and prayed so hard to join the elite crew. Instead, elementary teacher Christa McAuliffe was chosen to join the space crew.

Christa died 73 seconds after take-off on January 28, 1986.

And here's my third lesson – and I'll say this with some fun. At university, I once had this archaic and fastidiously measured professor in Biology 101 (chlorophyll, photosynthesis, frog dissection, LOL).

He'd come to class at the Science Centre spic and span with his usual checkered bowtie and black umbrella, looking like Jiminy Cricket. He'd go around the room looking over our shoulders to see if everyone was on the same page. And then he'd give a surprise test to determine if we were prepared. Sneaky chap, wasn't he? For the usual nerds, it was neat. But for us who came to class unprepared, we'd raise a howl and cry.

It's funny, but back in school, we got the lessons and the test – in that order. But in life, the test comes first, and then we learn the lesson.

But are we not all sitting in this great classroom in life, in a subject called Faith 101? Think about that.

We all are on a journey in this great enterprise we call life. It is a journey from Point A to Point B, with everything happening from C (first Crush) to Z (ending up with Zilch) between those points.

Whether we take the familiar road with a thousand others or the ones less traveled, still our journey is our own as we take our steps one at a time, one over the other. We all are going somewhere where we think we can find our purpose in life.

We liken this journey to a roller coaster ride with all the ups and downs, the twists and turns, and the sudden drops to the bottom. While the top can give us a great view of life, the sudden turns and dips and the lowest points give us the best lessons.

Sometimes, detours could suddenly block our path line, and we veer away from our destination by that force of circumstance. And yet, sometimes, we step on the brakes in the middle of the road, immobilized by fear, and then take a turn towards an even unfamiliar path simply because our gut tells us that there is nothing beyond that point.

Sometimes, it could be terrifying, but that's what life is all about. Scary because we do not know what lies ahead, and the unknown is always frightening. But life must go on for us the living, and like time, the direction is always clockwise, as we can never turn back the hands of time. Even with all the stops, detours, and sudden turns, there's no way to go but forward, at least in the grand scheme of things.

And there are no wrong turns in life, and here's why.

Wrong turns take us to where we are meant to be and where we should be, and the only reason I say it is not a wrong turn is that we are supposed to learn and grow from there and where that leads us.

The Greek mathematician Archimedes once said that the shortest distance between two points is a straight line. He is right. But only in geometry and if it is flat and linear. *But not in life.* Life is never linear but a tangled haywire of fantasy and reality, lies and truth, the ugly and the beautiful, ungodliness and divinity.

Your journey from Point A to Point B is never straight and never sure. I can tell you that it is fraught with so many surprises, dangerous curves and terrain, blind corners, and all.

The best way to keep moving is to enjoy the view and, while doing that, learn and grow ourselves into better people. Once the wheel turns, it goes on and on and never stops until we all reach our final destination, wherever we conceive that to be.

Now, here's a passage from 1 Corinthians.

It says, "When God took you out from there, you were a slave to man, but where God has put you now, you will bloom – It doesn't matter if you're still a slave for as long as you are a slave for God." So yes, I was a slave to my work back then, where Career was God. The moment I stepped out of my comfort zone, that was my first step at Point A.

When I came to Canada, it was all too simple. I was only looking for a new beginning and a better life. But look what I found. I found God - and on the way, found my family too.

Now, I am standing on my ground zero, called Point B. This is where I am and where I am supposed to be.

How about you? What is your Point B?

When people age and

lose the child in them,

they're good as dead.

Chapter Twenty-Five

The Child in Us

During my son Paolo's wedding to Philline, I was tasked to speak and give a toast as the groom's father. Although I was asked the day prior, I was never prepared even up to the moment I was called to do it. With all the preparations and excitement, it just didn't sink in. In hindsight, I'm glad I did not prepare, and let me tell you why.

The Friday afternoon wedding reception was held in the middle of a beautiful 130-acre vineyard called Vineland Estate Winery in the rolling hills of the Niagara escarpment. It is where you'll find some of the world's best wines: Cabernet Franc, Riesling, the rare Pinot Meunier, and the classic Chardonnay.

In an 1857 little stone house, all 36 family members gathered to celebrate the wedding. We drove early from Mississauga, leaving at 2:00 pm as it was a long weekend in Canada, with Monday being Labour Day. Canadians usually scramble towards the Niagara Rainbow Bridge by Friday afternoon and detoxify across the border until Monday. Traffic was horrendous, but our excitement made us unmindful of it. All we thought about was getting there before 4:00 pm and enjoy the warm and windy afternoon if we arrived early.

The bride's family was already there on the patio when we arrived. Summer chairs were carefully positioned on the grass by the stone cathedral as servers served cocktails. I managed to steal a pen (finally getting one that would write after two duds) and a yellow post-it for a draft of what I was to say for the toast.

I took a seat facing the excellent afternoon sun. I closed my eyes as my face enjoyed the gentle caress of the cool breeze. I did not want to miss the sun's warmth in its final days. It was now a threatened luxury as we held on to the coattails of summer. Soon it'll all be gone with autumn poised at the wings, ready to display her colors in full regalia. One could not help but close their eyes and bask in its magnificence.

I was about to begin writing when Philline's uncle Jun came over, and the usual small banter began. I soon discovered that, like me, he was a banker from back home in the Philippines. Then his wife Annabelle came to join us. As more people joined our group, I became lost in all the conversations.

As my turn came to speak that evening, I walked to the front nonchalantly. But quite the opposite, I was. The reality was that I was trying to gather my thoughts in every slow step that I made.

I began by thanking everyone for joining us at that moment. Then I honored my kids just so those gathered there would know Paolo and everyone in the family. I am so proud of my boys that I felt I'd waste the chance if I did not tell them how I felt when that moment was so perfect to say it. I knew it was Paolo's golden moment, and I did not want to steal his thunder, but I also knew that it was everyone's moment of pride and joy.

Although my eldest Popoy is my uncanny dead ringer, among my four boys, Paolo resembles what I am in many ways; I thus began.

He loves world history, and I do. He loves art, and I do love art. He is bohemian in many ways, and I am as well, although he takes it further. His Instagram and art portfolio handle is Deviant (this weighs a bit more). He plays the guitar and the piano, and I do. He would engage me in conversations about current events but often leave me clueless as I'd be ages back abreast.

For fun, I'd sneak up on him in his man cave to see what movie he's watching on his overhead projector, and I'd be surprised to find Japanese animè and Walt Disney. In turn, in my unguarded moments, he'd sneak up on me in our room and be surprised to see me watch Lion King.

I said I envied him for his view on life, seeing it from a child's eyes. For all his stockiness, a child lives deep in him.

I have always believed that the child in my soul has made me see things like no other, making it difficult for others to understand me. But over the years, through the most ruthless grind of things, I felt I had neglected that child. Drawn into the most inane games grown-ups play, I've been shoved down the fast lane of life, making me age beyond my time. And I say this because I forgot to feed the child in me. Carrying all the world's woes on your shoulders is the fastest way to age, faster than Charlton Heston in Planet of the Apes traveling at the speed of light and waking up 2,006 years later in a desolate New York City.

All of us have that child in us. The world will be a better place if we all see it through that child's eyes and be led in our bittersweet love affair with the ways of the world. Swiss Psychologist Jean Piaget has scientifically proven that children's worldview differs from adults. If only we could all come to that collective view, relationships with one another would be purer and uncomplicated.

Think about this: It is always very easy for the child in us to find joy and happiness in little things. Laughter and fun will be as natural as a child's smile. We would not overthink situations. We would not find malice in the actions of others. We would not easily take offense when things don't fall our way. We would find acceptance of others as easy as when a baby grasps our finger when we put it in their hand.

As people age and lose the child in them, they are good as dead. So, I say let the child in you remain. *Feed it.*

Feed it more than your bratty Ego. Feed it more than your drama king named Self-Pity. Feed it more than your Fears. Feed it more than your Self-Doubt. Because with negative emotions, it is the exact opposite. Negativity feeds off us. Like sponges, they drain all our strength and our love for life. Let them starve to death so you'll be happy - but feed the child in you, and you'll be happiest.

We can be anything we imagine if we just let the child take our hand and lead us to a whole new world. Matthew 18:10 says, "See that you do not despise these little ones. For I tell you that in heaven, their angels always see the face of my Father."

So, don't be afraid to be a child and act like a child. Regardless of your age, you are always young deep inside your shell. Be a Patch Adams to everyone with *Compassion* and *Humor* - two best friends who never fail to make the world a better place.

Clown out your day. Be the crazy you and be cool with it, just like Paolo - childish, daring, fun, and most of all – authentic.

I would not have said these things if I had written them down. But the fact that I did, unprepared and spontaneously, it could have come only from the child in my heart.

For a brief moment that night, perhaps the child in me held hands with the child in him.

In the end, it is your

hidden character that

will define you.

Chapter Twenty-Six

Victor Hugo and Me

Getting directions from our friendly Vietnamese front desk clerk Michel at our hotel was more straightforward than the Google map on our phones. He was articulate and knew the places one must visit while in Paris. Not wanting to sound so matter-of-factly, he loosened up and added tidbits of information - what's best to do and where to go for our first day in Paris. Although we were already in the trendy area south of Pigalle near the 9th Arrondissement where you'd see the museums, concert halls, and theatres such as the Garnier Opera, he offered a different must-see-must-visit area. It was not your usual touristy stuff but rather the kind an everyday bored Parisian might go and let loose. He gave us directions on where to get the best Parisian coffee al fresco, where to get the feel of a truly diverse community, and where the avant-garde would go to watch people who watch the avant-garde watch people. Then finally, he showed us where he'd spend his days off - the Les Marais District. It was once the preferred residences of the French nobility, including Cardinal Richelieu (I first heard this name from my brilliant professor in World History, Ralph Cecilio, God bless him wherever he is).

Not wanting to be touristy, we wanted to see something different. This time I Googled Les Marais. I discovered that it is the melting pot of artists, poets, the ageing elites, the gay, and people who'd spend their whole day drinking coffee. It is the closest thing to medieval Paris. It has a charm of its own, evoking festiveness and old romanticism. The streets are lined up with quirky boutiques and trendy shops.

Michel gave us a detailed sketch on a piece of paper on which subway trains to take to get to the place. Starting from Rue Lamartine, we walked towards the Notre Dame de Lorette and descended a flight of stairs to get to the train station.

The confusing and complex Metro train transfers in Paris would have been enough to make us give up and head back to the hotel, but this damnably intense surge of curiosity urged me to go on and keep looking.

Finally, we were able to locate the house of author Victor Hugo at the Place des Vosges. I wanted to know what else was behind the man who wrote The Hunchback of Notre Dame and Les Misérables. Beyond these great writings, I must admit I knew little of him, let alone what the public knows, although that would be too presumptive of me.

Well, we discovered he loved doing sketches and drawings, and his works of art are equally sublime as his writings. He also loved to do furniture decorating. And yes, he wrote lovely poems too.

But there was one thing that struck us.

Beyond the version that we know, he was also a doting grandfather.

Tragically, Hugo outlived all of his six children. He became the guardian of Charles' children after his premature death in 1871. He was particularly fond of George Walker, three years old and Margaret Rose, six months old.

In his poem The Art of Being a Grandfather, which he wrote in 1877 and one of his last writings before he died in 1878, he says, "There is no experience in life that can compare to being a grandparent. The joy is pure and simple; there are fewer expectations and agenda."

What I missed was knowing about Victor Hugo's other self – the private version.

In life, there is the Public You and the Private You. Johari's Window says there is a You that everybody knows (it is what we know as personality), but there is also a You that nobody knows but you (otherwise known as Character). Let's face it. What you are in public, you will be judged accordingly. Either you will be praised, or you'll be vilified.

The caveat here is: Keep the integrity of the Private You but don't let the Public You be shaped by others. Don't be swayed by anyone's opinion or judgment of you. It is never anyone's business to judge others; you allow them to take control of your life if you give in. What's to stop them next from directing your path they'd avoid themselves. The only exception I can think of is when their opinion says you will do far greater things in the future and points out your potential to do that. This way, you'd be more inspired to do better and soar higher, knowing that others see your value.

The only rightful judgment is reserved for your Maker. While we are wont to make judgments on ourselves, we are often wrong and often too unkind and exacting; we forget that our judgments of ourselves will not matter in the end. It is our Maker's that will.

Our propensity to judge others is even more preposterous. We think by what we see and hear for the general part, as our senses are too quick to lead us to judge. This predisposition is most unkind and uncharitable as it obscures the real character of the other person. We choose to believe what we like and then shut the door to everything else.

I know Ronald as the jolliest fellow in our neighborhood, but he is also the loneliest when he gets home. Loneliness descends upon him like a dark cloak as he closes the door behind him. That's the public and private side of him.

Natalie is strict and snobbish, but she is the most generous and charitable lady on her block as she feeds the hungry. Again, the public and the private Natalie.

David is unapproachable and often standoffish, but he has a gentle and kind heart and is most compassionate to the needy.

Often hidden by one's aversion to the public gaze, there is always a version of a person that is not seen - and it is by personal choice that it happens.

They like to remain private and invisible. Whatever their reasons are, it is always best to give them that tiny space.

I have friends who have made a difference in the lives of others for years, but nobody's heard of their deeds. They did not beat their chests and crow about it. No Facebook, Instagram, Twitter or Tik-Tok. They were beyond the cameras and the gaze of social media. But they love what they do – and that is character – always perceptible even when no one is watching.

This hidden version of the self is the most misunderstood, most ostracized, and most persecuted. Its silence and invisibility have often been perceived the wrong way, and every ugly adjective in Webster's has been thrown at it - passively aggressive, indifferent, sanctimonious - everything.

But hold it. Let us look beyond that veil of privacy. Behind the silent and invisible is a character no one knows. In the end, it is the hidden character that defines the man. So, what is Character, and how do we measure it?

Let me give you two ways to look at it -

1. To God, it is according to how you follow His two greatest commandments.

2. To mortals, it will always be relative - it is how you made their lives better.

And there's only one standard that I know of - *Goodness.*

Victor Hugo says it succinctly, "Our mind is enriched by what we receive. Our hearts by what we give. "

Bonjour!

We shape the world from

within ourselves long before

it shows its true face.

Chapter Twenty-Seven

The Prism of Life

Sometime in June of 2022, at Brussels Midi Central Station, we noticed a young man rummaging through the trash bins for food while waiting for our train for Amsterdam. Barefoot and hair disheveled, he was nonetheless, by all indications, in good health, but I could quickly tell he was famished. With the way he munched on a morsel of a doughnut, he must not have eaten since the 1944 Battle of the Bulge in Ardennes, some hour-and-a-half from there.

Moved by the scene, I unstrapped my backpack, took out a bag of mini croissants (must have been a dozen or so), and walked over to hand it to the young man. The glint in his eyes bared great joy as he took it from my hand, saying "Thank you" in accented English.

Having done the deed, I quickly turned around, heading back to Maria and the kids. "Pa, he jumped with joy as you walked away!" Leandro remarked.

Unsettled by the insignificance of my donation and his reaction, I did not want him to lose the momentum of his joy. I turned around with Leandro to give him my Birkenstock sandals.

“Where are you from?” I asked.

“I’m from Germany. Somebody stole my backpack with all my money and credit cards last Tuesday. I reported it to our embassy, and they said I should come back a few days later to see if the cards are re-issued”, he replied.

“Here are my sandals - wear these,” I told him as I unpacked my pair. “No, it’s okay. I still have my sandals, but I prefer to go barefoot. The station is so clean, and I like the feel of the floor walking with my bare feet.” How he enthused his response was so liberating. He said it like it was a pleasant discovery he would like to get accustomed to.

Now, that’s an answer I did not expect. The other perspective to what I thought was his great need.

Like a prism, we all see the same old world but yet see it differently when we turn the tube the way we want. We are wired differently, and our circuits diverge us into our uniqueness.

It’s the same with life.

German philosopher Immanuel Kant once said, "imagination is situated between our perception and understanding, that we do not see the world as it is; we see the world according to our instruments.” Seeing the same thing, even with a thousand eyes, may not seem to change its face, but each pair does according to how one feels towards it. We see the world through the eyes of our soul, and we shape it according to what we are within ourselves long before it shows its true face.

A long time ago, while waiting for our professor to arrive in one of my chemistry classes, I asked my classmates what they thought of a beautiful red rose in a vase on the teacher's desk. One said it reminded her of her first Valentine's Day present from one of her suitors. Another said it is what she always gets on her birthday. A guy said he hates roses because he once got pricked by their thorns. I said it reminded me of the red roses on my grandmother's casket at her burial.

What we think it is will become what it is, regardless of its face, size, shape, and content.

But to know a different view of it by others will beget twice greater the wisdom that we can behold if only we look at it their way. It only takes words like, "Oh, I see, yes." The more we come to know, the greater the wisdom they say, yet the greater we know, the more we discover that we know less.

And when we humbly admit that we know less, wisdom becomes more. The Greek philosopher Socrates says it profoundly, "The only true wisdom is knowing you know nothing." Such is the paradox of life.

Every day we randomly meet people who show us their view of life through their eyes. It is no coincidence. God meant it to be this way so we can all have perspectives of everything we come across. The more perspectives we behold, the nearer we are to seeing the face of truth. And the nearer we are to the truth, not too distant will be Beauty sitting gracefully by.

Truth and Beauty sit on the corners beside God on His throne.

And John Keats says it rightly so. Beauty is truth, and truth is beauty (Ode on a Grecian Urn).

God wants us to see life's true face through different eyes to give us a preview of what the other world is - that it is far superior to the one we have. We cannot see its magnificence differently but only through a heart perfectly fitted with pure love.

When I met the young man at the station, I said that life is viewed differently by one who needs to receive and by one who needs to give. To him, perhaps, life suddenly became different by misfortune when he was at the receiving end of mercy and compassion. But it also became distinct to me when I handed him my croissants, filling my need to reach out and give.

The measure of joy to both of us was the same - great was his need, but so was my compulsion to meet that need.

One act. Different needs.

Same joy.

The same intensity of emotions.

Both are a blessing - all in the prism of life.

As you walk down that lonely

road within yourself,

you will find the

secret to happiness.

Chapter Twenty-Eight

It's Okay to be Selfish

I know you reread the title. Now, read it again: It's okay to be selfish. No mistake.

I bought a Swiss watch because I like to feel good wearing it. I wear it once in a purple moon and keep it whirring in a self-winding cylinder 24/7; otherwise, it stops. I know you've bought yours too, and that's okay. It's okay to be selfish. Self-gratification! It makes me happy!

I drove more than a hundred kilometers to a small village in northern Ontario to buy a 1930s watch from an old veteran because I feel good knowing that I have one, and I like the feel of it on my wrist even if I have to wind it every 24 hours. A never-ending rewind which I don't mind. Self-gratification! It makes me happy.

I have a car I rarely use and have it in storage in my garage for more than half of the year. I save on mileage, gas, and insurance, but I like knowing I have it. (I know what you're thinking – "What a waste! Why don't you sell it!") But again, self-gratification! It makes me happy.

I painted our guests' washroom blood red and installed a grotesquely molded face of Joaquin Phoenix as the Joker on the wall, appearing like it's sticking out and looking at you while you sit on the throne. It looks so real - it scares the s**t out of my visitors who come to answer nature's call (oops, pun intended). Now it looks like a cheap prostitute's boudoir. Everyone in the house says it looks like a brothel they'd seen in old western movies. They don't like it, but again – Self-gratification! It makes me happy.

Weird, but it's who I am. And it is self-gratifying to me. It makes me happy. Selfish? Yes. These are the times that Selfishness, Hubris's twin, takes 90% of my body and soul. I'm not saying it's detestable. I am just driving a point here, so read on, and you'll discover that selfish acts can have twists. So, forget what I did because there are some selfish acts that are hardcore – and they draw others into it. They are the secret to your happiness.

Self-gratification is the name of the game this time. What makes you happy, do it! (Whoa! careful there!)

They wouldn't like this - and I could get in trouble, but my son Popoy and my daughter-in-law Yin have been sending *Balikbayan* boxes (strong cardboard boxes dimensioned 24X18X24 inches) with all used stuff, clothes, jackets, shoes, toys and what have you, to Cebu in the Philippines where it is distributed to those in need by Yin's siblings. It's a lot of work, and they pay a lot for air freight, but they do it nevertheless because it makes them happy. These past few years, they have bought slippers, school bags, crayons, pencils, notebooks and used children's books to be given during Yin's birthday to street kids. They never talk about it, but it's always done there. During the last Covid times, in the days of autumn, the family would go and buy a trunkful of McDonald's breakfast and let their kids give these out to the homeless in the streets. The dad told me everyone always feels good and happy on the way home, especially the kids.

My friends Philip and Ellen go home to Cagayan de Oro on Philip's birthdays and bring toys, clothes, and books to the kids at the Boy's Town Orphanage in their city. They think nobody knows about it, but I do. His birthdays never seem to be happier than when they do this. They've done this great deed even while still in the country.

My boys have a tall glass box facing our front door marked: "For the Needy." In it are coins and Canadian dollar bills that pile up over time. All to buy McDonald's breakfasts and warm blankets for those in need on the streets.

Why do we all give? It is because it makes us feel good inside. Self-gratification! It makes us happy. It is who we are. It is our core. Albert Einstein once said, "We know from daily life that we exist for other people first of all, for whose smiles and well-being our happiness depends."

The most selfish thing you can ever do in this world is to help someone else. Why? Because it comes back to your core. It comes back to your whole being *because you want to make yourself happy.* Without you realizing it, it is you becoming you.

Even the destitute and poorest man can make himself happy by giving others what little he has without regard if he's even needier than his recipient. If they can do it, imagine how many could be happy if all the rich and powerful reach out. Imagine what their wealth and power can do and how many could benefit from it. If we realize that it is not how much we have but what we do with what we have that matters, then the world will be better. And I say there is no expiry in doing good, so there's still a chance to make this world better. Elon Musk doesn't need to move to Mars.

We always have the opportunity to do something bigger than ourselves. Going beyond what we think we cannot do will unleash even more power and strength that we don't know we already have. And if we believe that the world is going to the dogs, we don't know much then. Some people go under the radar and in silence to make the world better, one step at a time.

So, look into your soul. Are you one of those people? When you walk on that lonely road within yourself, deep within the core of your being, you will find the secret to happiness – your happiness.

As you read this, you smile because I know you've been doing your share to make this world a little happier in your little way – silently and anonymously. *Nobody else knows!* But that's okay because the rewards are not here anyway. Only credit cards give you the Airmiles and bonuses here.

The fact that nobody knows you're doing it means you're doing great on Somebody's scorecard. And that's how it should be. Again, it is okay to be selfish. So, go and make yourself happy.

Give.

When you say, "God bless you,"

you are unleashing God's favor

towards others.

Speak it now.

Chapter Twenty-Nine

Speak the Blessing

As my son Leandro got out the door the other day and went to his car for work, I followed him. Unaware that I did, he was surprised to see me tap on the window on the passenger's side. As he rolled it down, I asked him, "Have you forgotten anything?"

Immediately though mumbled, he recited the Book of Numbers prayer, "May the good Lord bless you and keep you..."

I said, "You forgot your wallet!" As I handed it to him, I spoke the same prayer he had given me. It was plain to see he was stressed. His co-worker was on vacation, and he'd be taking the extra work in his stead. But through that anxiety, he still spoke the blessing.

We all need blessings. And we all need to speak it now!

I have recently listened to one great pastor - Joel Osteen. He stands out among the best in the world, probably next to the Reverend Billy Graham. Their way of talking about the goodness of the Lord has drawn people of all ages, perhaps because people find a great connection in the way they passionately profess their faith in their engagement with the listening world. Both speak with a fiery passion. I remember him talking about blessings changing the face of the world - if only it is expressed as often as we can and to as many people as we can, he says, the world will become different. The way he highlighted this need resonated in me that it stopped me in my tracks and gave me serious thought about it.

All of us have people in our lives who need our blessing. We all need validation and approval. We need somebody in our life to tell us that they love us and that we are needed. Many of us are grounded in self-doubt and low self-esteem, and like ships, we can be stuck and anchored forever, unable to sail toward our dreams unless a blessing frees us.

Social media has subliminally created a standard about how we are supposed to look and live our life that we often look at ourselves in the mirror and ask, "Am I okay?" It has made it easy for people to find out if they're in or out. Suddenly you see friends' activities, and you don't get invited. You begin to self-doubt the quality of your life as you compare it with your friend's post – looking like she is romping on the red carpet at some Oscar awards. A study made by a social media group at the University of Michigan in 2013 that tracked Facebook users over two weeks concluded that they were less satisfied with their lives, even to the point of undermining them. They felt that they had to "keep up" with the trends. There was the creeping urge to turn Facebook into a platform of one-upmanship. So again, you may ask, "Am I okay, still?"

Of course, we're all okay. If we compare ourselves to others, we don't seem okay and think we are the worst, even on our best days. We can only compare ourselves with ourselves. The only person we should try to outdo is the person we were yesterday. And sometimes, we get stuck in a hard place simply because we need a good word to pull us out.

With the same weight as God's blessings, our prayers to our children would mean much more than if they were to come from others. When they hear it from us and others whom they look up to and respect, it will make a world of difference in their day.

When you say to your child – "I'm so happy with how you're living your life. You're a good son, and I'm so proud of what you did today. You're going to have a great future because you're a smart and strong person" – you just spoke the blessing and released God's favor into their future.

When you tell your spouse, "As the days go by, you are becoming so beautiful, I love you so much, and I'm so glad I married you. You mean so much to me" – you just released God's blessings towards her.

When you say to your brother, "You are doing so great; I admire your honesty and hard work. I am so happy we are friends". Those are not just kind and polite words. You're not just being friendly or considerate. You just released God's favor into their life. You don't realize it, but when they say it to others, you have just started a ripple of goodness in the world. Imagine the exponential impact it's going to do when you start it.

The moment you speak the blessing, you have just stirred the power within them to become a better version of themselves, lifting them from the ground to step up to the next level. Your blessing will unleash God's favor into them like a wind into their sail toward their destiny. When you say your blessing, you release God's abundance, protection, grace, and wisdom over their lives and future. Your words shape their destiny.

And what does it take? Let me tell you: it doesn't take much!

One word of kindness. One word of encouragement.

One "God bless you."

And that's all. You've just set the sails of their lives.

After graduating from college, I flew to the big city for training in banking. Coming from a small province, I've never seen as many buildings taller than my university's 5-Storey Science Centre. I was led into an elevator to our 19th-floor training room for the first time on my first day. Inside the lift, my trainer directed me with her eyes to a gentleman at the front and whispered to my ear to take a close look at him. When we got down on our floor, she said the guy earns 65,000 pesos a month.

I shrunk. I just signed my contract for 700 pesos a month.

In the training room, when everyone introduced themselves, I swear I could have fit into a jar with Tom Thumb or Rick Moranis in the movie Honey, I Shrunk the Kids. They were all tops of their class at school and were *cum laude.* And there I was, the guy with the *loudest* heartbeat in the room. The only decent shadow still standing and holding me down on my spot was a recommendation by my provincial bank manager to be included in that class – aside from the scare of reimbursing the high fee I'd pay back if I quit the training. He believed in me and what I could become, even if I thought I lacked the capability.

It was my first time to be away from home. Imagine my sense of insecurity. One day, I received a letter from my father in the mail. When I read it, I thought it was a forgery. I could not believe my eyes. I read it over and over again. It was not the usual him because we rarely sat down and talked as he was always busy in government. For the longest time, I had wished for his approval and encouragement. But he was just not there; if he was, his mind and spirit were away.

In the letter, he said my mother and my sister, and he missed me so much they could not wait to see me do great things in the future. He ended the letter with this:

"We love you; bring home the bacon!"

Always playing smart-alecky, I thought, "Oh yeah, bacon?! Bacon and egg Sandwich?"

I looked it up in the dictionary at the training room library. It was an idiomatic expression that changed my life.

It meant – *Go, achieve success.*

What he did was speak the blessing into my future. When we graduated, I delivered the address on behalf of the class. And the rest is history.

Now, let me ask you. Do you speak the blessing to your children? Do you speak the blessing to your spouse? To your co-workers? To your friends?

Well, you can tell me, "Bob, I told my wife I loved her when we married 20 years ago!"

Fine. You can put this book down now, call and tell her "I love you" for the second time today. It's never too late. You have to say to her every day that she is special. That she is loved and that she means so much to you.

My dad used to send love letters and flowers to my mom for no reason other than perhaps his way of saying he was thinking of her. I've known friends who have never said "I Love You" to their spouses. This lack of loving assurance may be why many couples are mired in everlasting fights, depression, and misery. After the honeymoon, their love life just flatlined. Instead of lifting each other, they squandered their days by bickering and arguing. One word of love may have changed everything, but sadly, the chance was missed.

Every time I'd call my mother on the phone half a world away and tell her, "God bless you; I'm not there to take care of you, but may the Lord take care of you on my behalf," She'd be silent on the other end. Still, I knew she'd feel better because the next time I called her, I could hear her play the piano in the background as her caregiver answered the phone. One time she phoned me, frantically saying a burglar may have tried to enter her house the night before. I told her to open her Bible on Psalm 91 and leave her front door open for the night – and not worry. "Are you crazy?" She scoffed at it, but a few days later, she called again, asking me what Bible passage it was again. I said, "Psalm 91, God bless and protect you!"

Withholding back the blessing causes untold misery in people, and for years this causes them to get lost in the maze of life and never find their way out of it. Even today, people get old and die without hearing a blessing come their way since birth. Their self-worth has never gone past their notional value. You may tell me that's just how they are, and they're fine even without it, but imagine if they got the blessing and where they'd be today. We'll never know until we've given it and until they hear it.

Some children go through this ordeal for their entire life simply because they never got blessings from their parents or anyone. They were not "good enough" than their other siblings or played soccer well enough in school, or their grades were not good enough to meet their folk's expectations, or better than dad's when he was in school. They were just not as good as the kid next door.

As parents, you know it doesn't cost you anything to speak it. It's as easy as getting a packet of peanuts and a sundae cream at a fast-food chain drive-thru. Don't withhold the blessing in you. When you get the first chance, speak your blessings to your children. Tell them how much you love them. Tell them how proud you are of them. Your words will unleash God's favor into their future.

Now, you might say your kids are now grown up and think it's too late. Well, goodness doesn't have an expiry date, and its supply never ends. It lasts a whole lifetime. You can start now and re-direct their paths.

Joel Osteen gave us a great story about withholding blessings. He says there was this guy named Robert. He had an alcoholic father, and they lived in a small town where everybody knew everybody. Everyone in his village knew his father as the town drunkard.

On the contrary, his son Robert was a football star who made it to the high school and college All-American teams. Football was his life, and he poured every cell in his body to excel at it. But as far as he knew, his father had never watched him play even one single football game. His father never told him how great he was and never cared. For a long time, Robert longed for his father's encouragement and approval.

He found out years later that his dad was actually in a few of his games and that he watched from the farthest part of the bleachers, where he'd remain unnoticed. He was scared somebody would recognize him and point him out, saying, "look, there's the star player's drunkard dad!"

After Robert's college days, he became a successful pastor and became famous. One day, he got a call from the town hospital saying his father had a heart attack and that he might not make it. He put everything down and rushed to the emergency room to see his father. When he came in, he saw his father all tubed up. One moment he would be conscious; the next, he's not. Now, Robert silently sat down by his bedside and held his hand. He thought Robert was the doctor. He said something to Robert that forever changed his life.

He said, "Hey Doc, have I ever told you about my son Robert? I'm so proud of him. He's so talented and gifted, and so many people love him. He was a great football player, and now he's a pastor of a great church. God, I wish I'd see him again, and I also hope you can meet him."

That day, Robert heard the words he had longed to hear for more than 30 years.

He finally received the blessing from his father. It was like filling a void in his heart that only his father could fill – like a gust of wind that lifted the wings of his soul, he felt healed and empowered.

We must understand that love remains just a word until it is expressed and given away. A gift is not a gift until it is given. A blessing is not a blessing until it is spoken. For years, the father had the blessing locked inside him that he never released. He never spoke it out.

Now, what does this mean to us? Look into your heart. In that crowded space, wanting to come out and change somebody's life is a blessing. There is a blessing only you, as a parent, can give. My dad was not so expressive and affectionate to me, although I knew he loved me and showed it in many ways. It might not have been a kiss on the cheek, it could have been a kick in the butt, but he loved me, I'm sure. And he said it only once in my life – in that letter he wrote to me. It could be the same for you. People express their love and feelings in so many ways, but there is nothing as good and fulfilling as a blessing said with love.

Some of you might not be affectionate or expressive with your feelings and don't do that stuff; you can be as dry as a bone saying, "That's not the way we are. No, we don't do that in our family. We don't talk; we're not used to sweet talking. We don't hug; we don't say I love you."

Well, that's okay. But there is always a first time.

You have to tell yourself – "This is a new day. I will start to speak the blessing. Today, I will say *I love you* to my spouse. Today, I will tell my son and daughter, *"I'm so proud of you and what you have become."* Today, I will tell my co-worker, *"I am happy working with you."* Today, I will whisper in my son's ear, "*You will do great things in the future.*" Then, watch what happens as God takes over.

I am astonished that with kind words, we can actually change somebody else's life and their direction. Every time we say God bless you to somebody, we know we release God's favor toward the person. We might not see the difference right away, but it will come. A drop of water constantly dripping on a stone can hollow out a hole.

As you read these lines, I know there is that itch in you to bless those you love. You have a blessing locked up on the inside that somebody desperately needs. Dare to release it, not just once, but repeatedly until they get it. Like the stone, they will eventually receive the blessings they need.

Regardless of the kind of people we need to give it to, we must do it. We don't size them out first and decide if they're deserving of the blessings or not. If we do that, we're missing the whole point. The more we think they don't deserve it, the more we should give it.

The apostles were not perfect. They were the original version of Robert Aldrich's 1967 film The Dirty Dozen. They were a weird and strange mix. Yet, for all their faults and quirks, Jesus valued them and spoke the blessing to them. One day, He just looked them straight in the eye and said, "*You are the light of the world; you are the salt of the earth.*" He spoke the blessing. When they heard these words, they did not leave Jesus' side till the end. Putting it another way, Jesus was saying, "I'm happy to be your friend. I'm proud of you, and you are special to me. You have the power in you to change the world!" True enough, they have changed the world into the one that we know today.

Jesus believed in them just as that provincial bank manager believed in me in my mediocrity when he recommended me for training. Jesus spoke by faith to the apostles and called forth their potential, which had struck them deep at their very core.

All told, they were not anything special. They were just ordinary folks. But when Jesus said a blessing to them, they rose to their potential and shaped their destiny. They rose to the level of what Jesus saw in their future.

I'm no freaking genius. I was everybody's funny and mediocre classmate who slept in class after lunch. I was your average guy who skipped classes to go and watch movies and prowl on pretty girls school. I still feel I got away with the biggest heist in my career. I flunked my math in high school and took a summer make-up course for it, yet for the life of me, I am still figuring out why I ended up in a job with food-catered meetings in a swanky boardroom in a skyscraper. I flunked my algebra, yet I could mentally count percentages and get the answers quickly before anyone could punch the last digits in their calculators. It is a blessing I still cannot believe I have received up to this day – unexplainable, I tell you. But I figured out that it could be because I took to heart the blessings my father gave me a long time ago. It is because my manager believed in me and yanked out the sleeping confidence in my soul. For all the odds Abraham Lincoln faced as a youth growing up in a log cabin, he once said, *"I'm a success today because I had a friend who believed in me, and I didn't have the heart to let him down."*

What am I saying? When you speak the blessing; when you call out a person's potential; when you look at someone in the eye and say, "I don't just see you for what you are, I can see beyond what you are today. Your best is yet to come", your words will shape their destiny. They will rise to the level of what you tell them they can be.

To see a miracle in somebody else's life, speak your blessing. If you want to make a difference in somebody else's life, give a word of kindness and encouragement - it will predict greatness in their future.

Osteen spoke about a 5-year-old boy named Michael who had just discovered his mother was pregnant with a baby girl (because she told him). Michael was so excited he could not wait to see his baby sister. Every morning, he would put his head on his mother's tummy, close his eyes and listen to the heartbeat, gently singing to his little sister –

"You are my sunshine, my only sunshine.

You make me happy when skies are gray

You'll never know, dear, how much I love you

Please don't take my sunshine away."

Week after week, month after month, he would continue to sing it hundreds and hundreds of times. The mom finally went into the hospital to have the baby, but there were some complications in the delivery. Sadly, the baby did not do well, and the doctors said there was very little chance she would survive. Michael's mom and dad were so heartbroken as they saw the nurse take the baby into the Intensive Care Unit of the Neo-Natal section. Michael did not understand what was happening when he saw all the commotion. He just kept asking his mom when he could see his baby sister.

As the hours went by, the doctors returned with the grim news that the baby might not probably make it through the night. The mother was so anguished looking at Michael and then realized that if he did not see his baby sister that night, he might never see her alive again. It was now or never. Even though no children were allowed in the Intensive Care Unit, she snuck Michael in when the Head Nurse was not watching.

For the first time, Michael finally got to see his baby sister. He was scared as he saw all the wires, tubes, and electrical gadgets around his little sister.

At about that time, the Head Nurse saw them and said – "Hey, what's that child doing there? He has to leave right now!"

All of a sudden, without the mother saying a word, little Michael put his hands on the little glass crib and started singing to his baby sister,

"You are my sunshine, my only sunshine.

You make me happy when skies are gray

You'll never know, dear, how much I love you

Please don't take my sunshine away."

The Head Nurse noticed that the baby's rapid heart rate began to stabilize. She said to Michael – "Keep on singing."

And Michael continued –

"You are my sunshine, my only sunshine.

You make me happy when skies are gray

You'll never know, dear, how much I love you

Please don't take my sunshine away."

After several minutes, the nurse just stood there and watched with amazement as the baby's heart rate came down to normal. Her pale blue face began to glow and became peaceful, and there was a sweet smile on her little face. As Michael's singing continued, God's miraculous blessing came upon his baby sister. The long and short of it was that the baby came home normal after a few days. There is incredible power in our words when we speak the blessing.

As you come upon these lines, I want you to pause and think about it.

Is there someone that needs your blessing today? You may not need to look beyond the four walls of your house. Speak it. Speak it now.

Then watch what happens.

God bless you.

Smile – it's the cheapest

way to stay young!

Chapter Thirty

Robert and Me

I have no hang-ups about looking old. I hardly think about it, although my body wants to punch the nose of the guy making those funny faces in front of my mirror in the mornings. I was astounded reading about the costs people spend to stay young.

I've seen the cover of a book written and co-authored by the 92-year-old Gloria Vanderbilt with her equally famous son. She could easily pass off to be a 40-year-old, but hey, she has the money. According to a US News article, for hair - women spend US$75 every five weeks; an Anti-aging skin care regimen would cost US$50.00 to $150.00 max a month. For teeth, it is a whole range of enhancements like whitening, veneer, and implants, of which the latter's cost is about $30,000. Then we have Botox, eyelid surgeries, breast implants, and tummy tucks. All in all, it is a hefty fortune, depending on which seat you're on.

I have a good friend named Robert who stands out tall among my many friends. What separates him from the rest is his smile.

Quite intrigued, I asked myself what could it be that makes him such a happy person. I say, there's not a time I haven't seen him without his smile. It always makes me think his smile is the cheapest thing he'd wear each day. Freely given to all, I'd say he has the heart of a child in him. From all that I've seen, it appears that the world never seems to affect that smile, and in fact, it may have been the other way around – changing the world, or at least his little sphere of it – by that smile.

Maria and I were invited to his 60th birthday not too long ago and were a bit surprised that he would be *that* age. We had always thought he was way younger than that.

His family and friends from all over came to the party. As the night wore on and the karaoke singing slowed down, each of his friends came up to the front to give a verdict. I had expected either a pat on the back or a kick in the rump (and there's only eighteen inches difference between them). Gatherings like this usually have the celebrant come home bruised, battered, and tattered.

But not Robert.

As each one took their turn to say something about him, I was amazed at all the heaps and praises. They all spoke about how Robert had helped them when they first arrived as new immigrants. From meeting them at the airport to settling them down to picking them up at the curve when they had no car. Small things indeed, but so terrific and memorable they touched the hearts of many. As each one said their piece, there was no let up about the goodness of his heart. So again, good deeds, like happy things, live forever.

Beyond that, what astonished me was that the people that Robert and his wife Mai helped over the years returned the favor *forward* to others – in the same way they had received it. Unbeknownst to the couple was that they had started a ripple of goodness in their community of friends. That night, they heard how their good hearts touched many. To this day, years down, the wave continues.

It took Robert 60 years to hear how many loved him. Yet many people die without knowing they are loved, if at all.

Now, my questions are answered.

Robert and all his ways of helping others - make him happy simply because that is how he is.

And that's why he always smiles. It has become his logo.

And his smiles make him younger than the age we just celebrated. All these things add up.

Life doesn't always give you the answers quickly and straight.

But smiles are *curves* on your face that make everything *straight*.

Now I know why.

If today you need something

to do in the name of love -

just do it!

Chapter Thirty-One

The Eleventh Hour

On the morning of **January 17, 1977**, in Utah State Prison, 36-year-old criminal Gary Mark Gilmore was going to die by firing squad. He had demanded the implementation of his death sentence after moral arguments had held off the death penalty. He was to become the first criminal to be executed after ten years.

He was leather-strapped to a chair with a wall of sandbags behind him to trap the bullets. Five local police officers stood concealed behind a curtain with five small holes, just enough through which they aimed their rifles.

When asked for any last words, Gilmore said, *"Let's do it."*

The Roman Catholic prison chaplain gave him the last rites. Gilmore, now cloaked with a black hood, uttered his last words to the chaplain. *"Dominus vobiscum,"* to which the chaplain replied, *"Et cum Spiritu tuo."* It means "The Lord be with you – and also with you."

They say those who wait to repent until the eleventh hour die at ten thirty. But not this one. Gilmore died at the appointed hour. There was no stay of execution.

His last words were more of a battle cry to get things done.

Ten years later, in 1987, the smart guys at Nike advertising picked this up with a little twist. Inspired by its bravado, they reworded it, and the rest is history.

Now, emblazoned beside the Nike swoosh is the challenge – *Just do it!* It has become a philosophy of life to many, resonating even with the non-athletic class.

What I'm going to talk about this time is not about repenting. It is about doing the things we must do simply because they must be done. Just take away the reasons why and - do it.

We need to take care of things in our life immediately. A leaking faucet. A clogged drain. A broken fuse. A broken heart. A sick child. A broken relationship. As we wrestle with a thousand and one things that fight for our attention, we must carefully sift and prioritize which ones we need to attend to right away. Affairs of the heart and soul take the front seat. All other matters need to wait.

People are slow learners, especially about the value of time, and they've been so sloppy about this since time began (pun in there). Time is the only commodity every man has in common, whether rich or poor, young or old.

Now I can say that I have one thing in common with Elon Musk or Jeff Bezos and everything else they can have, and I won't mind. Remember that we are always the Defending Champions of our own time; if we lag, it will overtake us to create an upset. Time waits for no one, so we must catch up with its pace.

To illustrate, here's a classic upset where time may have worked against a clear winner. Roger Federer lost to Ukrainian Sergiy Stakhovsky in the Wimbledon finals in 2013. Federer was the defending champion, but Sergiy was 116th in the world. So, we must be on our toes, race up to pace, and play our game well; otherwise, we will get caught – and it happens in our most unprepared and vulnerable moments.

Montreal-based geologist and cartoonist Jacques Goldstyn wrote a children's book called The Eleventh Hour. It is about two childhood friends, Jim and Jules, who were born 2 minutes apart in the same village. Their two-minute gap became a prominent pattern in their day-to-day life as they grew up. When the young men were drawn to the first World War in Europe, the usual pattern continued with Jim always getting things done ahead of Jules, who was always two minutes behind. Sent to France, the boys cemented their friendship as the rigors of war put them together in the most horrific situations – foggy frontlines, muddy and cold trenches, rat-infested bunkers, and hunger. Through it all, Jim had been the faster and stronger one – always ahead of Jules in almost all endeavors.

In the early and foggy morning of November 11, 1918, the boys were sent out to the front for one last push. As usual, Jim was the first to climb over the trenches.

He gets shot at 10:58 and dies in Jules' arms.

Two minutes later, the war ended as the armistice began at 11:00 that day.

But the story does not end there. The author follows Jules into Canada, where he spent his remaining years as a clockmaker. Keeping his best friend always in his heart, he had set all his clocks 2 minutes behind the eleventh hour.

When I last visited my ailing mother in 2011, I asked her if she had forgiven her biological brothers and sisters for all they may have done to her and if she had asked for their mercy and forgiveness for what she may have done to them. As I waited for her reply, she merely shook her head, probably bewildered by my impudence.

I looked her in the eye and said, "You're going to live up to a hundred and fifty." She looked away and stared out the window.

A year later, I asked her the same question on the phone. This time she said yes.

A few months later, she passed on.

All of us have time on our hands. All of us have Forgiveness in our hearts.

Forgiveness and Time have always played their roles as partners in human relations. More often, it is Time alone that moves ahead without Forgiveness as when we hold on and carry our grudges. When we withhold it, we surrender in hope to what we believe Time can handle. But often, Time does not heal, and people die without reaping its benefits. But when we give Forgiveness away, we reset Time to return and find what was lost. Only when it is given out and accepted will Time move forward again.

The consequences of my mom's forgiving will never be known as feelings are hard to deal with, let alone fathom. It will be easy to discern for the living as actions will always talk. But for her - the departed, her Maker will judge it. I now wonder whether forgiveness took her on a different course to another destination. Who knows.

There is no such thing as the eleventh hour because every hour is an appointed hour; it is just that we don't pay attention. So, if you need to do something for yourself or a loved one today, just do it. It could be your last straw or theirs.

Remember that in the end, whatever you think, say, or do, everything is within an appointed time, and the most important thing to consider is the one that matters the most - your answer to the question if you have loved or have forgiven others – regardless of where time finds you.

So again, just do it. Your hour is now.

To be brave, truthful, and

unselfish. All these, I pray

upon a star.

Chapter Thirty-Two

My Grown-up Jiminy Cricket

Pinocchio does not have the monopoly of a Jiminy Cricket – that bug, that flamboyant boulevardier, monsieur flâneur, and gentleman of the leisure.

In this humdinger of a children's tale about a pinewood boy named Pinocchio, Jiminy Cricket is his "conscience" who takes care of him as he walks on the road to self-discovery. Jiminy was to show the wooden boy the difference between good and evil, as he had promised the Blue Fairy to make Pinocchio a brave, truthful and unselfish boy.

I was probably not older than seven when my mother bought me this "A Little Golden Book" story of Pinocchio. As kids, we all had our Jiminy Crickets. As I grew into adulthood, Jiminy Cricket's voice became distant and fainter as I listened more to my own – trying hard to carve my wood of identity. While I continued my quest to be brave, truthful, and unselfish, I failed. By the time I was 30, my nose would have gone around the world twenty times twenty.

With the loud cacophony of voices fighting for my attention, not a few times did I listen to the wrong voices in my life. It did not help that I was raised and schooled in a strictly Jesuit environment from grade school to law school. I still had the freedom to choose which voice I'd listen to, and I've always known that voices come in different guises - the pure, the sultry, and the rough; but any voice, for that matter, will not always be what it may seem. The evil one is a good ventriloquist, constantly throwing out a convincing line from the friendliest-looking marionettes. Like a slippery slope, it could slide us down the wrong paths in life if we're not careful and discerning enough.

I finally met an old friend when I joined a weekend retreat called Daze (Weekend) with the Lord. Out of the darkness and onto the light, I finally found my true version of Jiminy Cricket – my "conscience" - the Divine Spirit.

It has no self-interest other than my own, and it has no other task but to see me through the correct path of life – that Road Within myself. Today, while I continue my search for courage, truthfulness, and being a man for others, I unceasingly look up to this friend - for His voice and guidance.

In everything I do, I press my ears hard upon my inner chambers to find it and distinguish the pure noise from the right and perfect decibel of truth. And in that voice, He generously arms me with the burning flame of faith, the eternal spring of hope, and the all-powerful and disarming battle cry of love and forgiveness as I face my daily battles.

Our daily walk on our Road to Damascus is so laden with so many struggles we need nothing less than a voice that points to the right way, the truth, and life.

That gentle voice has always been faithful to us and has been there since we were a child. As we grew into the persons we are today, He's also grown with us - all too patient and forgiving, even if we did not listen to him well enough over the years.

So, be still and listen to His voice.

If size mattered,

the elephant would be

king of the jungle.

Chapter Thirty-Three

The Mustard Seed

In 2008, we moved to Canada. Jobless for over a year, I was finally given a break in 2010 when Canada's largest bank, asset-wise, hired me. Today, it is still the largest in assets (2022) and within the Global 100.

Two weeks into the job, I was given a $750,000 Single Borrower Limit (SBL) credit authority. This means I can approve credit applications of a single entity aggregately up to that amount. This pales to my 2 million Philippine Peso SBL back home (roughly translated to $47,600 compared to its equivalent of 31.5 million Philippine Pesos now thrown into my discretion).

Typically, my 8-hour shift would have me act (approve or disapprove) on 48 accounts – all coming from eastern Canada up to the Maritimes. That is precisely one account every 10 minutes if without a break. Like the Forrest Gump box-of-chocolate thing, I wouldn't know what kind of credit application would pop up next on my screen when I click the 'next' button. There was the simple credit card application, the car loan, the line of credit, the home mortgage, the home equity line of credit, construction loans, and the complex bridge financings. I would usually do an average of 65 applications, all subject to my risk tolerance feel. Although there was no room for emotional play on the applications as everything was boxed-in and measured, there were gray areas that made you pause and think.

Questions like: What is the reason for the need? What is the applicant going through? Sometimes, spending patterns tell a lot more than just the numbers. I'd get a snapshot of a personal profile by looking at the numbers and patterns in how people use their money. But as long as the ratios and credit score indexes were in place, they were actionable - all in a day's work.

One day, just before lunch, as I clicked on "next," an application for a $6,000 personal loan popped up on my screen. On the top tab was the reason: "To visit my sick father in the Philippines. Cancer". I read the name, age, status, and occupation. Then I read it back over again.

I paused. I leaned back on my chair.

She was a caregiver. Like many Filipinos who come to Canada, they leave their homes, families, husbands, and children to care for the elderly Canadians. The sad irony is that she had an ailing (perhaps dying) father back home whom she could not even physically reach out to and care for because of financial restraints while caring for the elderly in Canada. The endorsing branch credit manager was perhaps moved by the reason for the application when he included unnecessary information about the ailment - Cancer. Okay, I get it, I said to myself.

But all the ratios were pretty bad. She had about four open credit cards unused and a couple more with low credit limits, which were maxed out. I stared at the application for a while as my mind raced to act on it within 10 minutes. My eyes were all over the screen, tweaking all the numbers to get a tolerable ratio. I removed my finger from the 'disapproved' button and picked up the phone. I called up the endorsing branch credit manager.

I said, "I'm calling about the $6,000 application of Pilar de la Cruz (not her real name). You have to talk to her. Tell her you must close all the open credit cards, tuck in one card's outstanding balance into the new loan, and pay off another one. But I'd increase the loan amount so you can apply the excess of $6,000 to close the other account. She would have a lower payback amount. I want to see good ratios when you send it back. I'll park this in my queue, and you call me before 4:00. I'm off at 4:30."

At 4:15, my phone rang, and it was him. I told him to open the file on his end while I opened it on my screen. True enough, all the ratios fell into place except for the total debt service ratio, which was up by about 2 points above the bank's threshold; but it would fall on my tolerance risk. "I can live with that," I said to myself. After a minute, I said, "This is good; I'll work on this now." Then I hung up.

As I gently put my finger on the Approve button, I held my breath and said to myself, "Now, you can go home."

Click!

"I hope you'll still catch him."

I can unflinchingly do the $750,000 limits per application, breeze through the 'next' button, and shall have approved a total of $36.0 million in a day. But this $6,000 made me sit back on my chair and pause. It was a relatively small amount, but there was something to it that tugged at the heart.

One of the paradoxes of life is that as we keep building things on top of the other, we seem to view size as a measure of grandness and accomplishment. The propensity to equate this with power suddenly becomes a norm. Grand-scale deeds and events attract attention, making it an end goal in all undertakings. I don't see it that way. If size really mattered, then here's a funny analogy that might drive home my point - it would be the elephant who should be the king of the jungle, not the lion. But it's not as simple as this.

While I agree that bigger endeavors and broader applications favor many, the small things still matter. It is the small things that the individual can still grasp on his level, not the bigger things. Small things are just easy to keep in their pockets.

At the start, when I cited the ranking, size, and might of the banks I've worked with, I was highlighting the possibilities they can actually do for the greater good of all and many. But it was also to bring to the fore that if they can do big things, they can also do small things. What I mean here are the small things they can do that will mean almost *nothing* to them but could be *everything* to some. When you have nothing, anything will be something, and that something could be everything.

I am reminded of the gospel of Matthew 13:31-32 about the grain of mustard seed. This seed is one of the smallest in the Middle East, but when it is sown in the most fertile soil and nurtured, it can become the greatest and mightiest - and when likened to faith, it can move mountains. Based on this parable, something happened between the seed sown on the ground and the mountains moving.

It was *Faith*.

Even when someone thinks he can only do something small, it becomes enormous when combined in the grand scheme. It may be insignificant in the eyes of men, but not in God's. Same thing with the gospel of Luke 16:10 when Jesus said, "He that is faithful in small things is also in much."

When I paused on that account, I knew the ratios were way off. I also knew it was nothing against all the huge amounts that passed through my fingers that day. But I had faith in what I was about to do – and that was what happened somewhere between the small insignificant click of the mouse and Pilar de la Cruz's flight back to the Philippines. It was the heart holding down the heavy hand of the mind for a moment.

Some things do not belong to gray areas. Being high and mighty does not mean one cannot bend down and pick up a fallen brother. Being fast and strong does not mean one cannot slow down and wait for the infirm struggling to catch up with you. Being involved in a thousand things does not imply a single thing is not worth your sweat; remember that it is still part of the thousand. I knew that it was a small shot and that it was *nothing* in a day's work. But somewhere, to someone, it was *everything.*

When I came home later that day, I spoke to Maria.

I started with, "I just did something I'm happy about today."

Taking out a tray of chocolate brownies from the oven, she carefully sliced out a small piece for me – insignificantly just bitesize when she could have given me a bigger chunk.

I was so hungry, the small piece mattered.

She smiled. She knew.

There are only two ways to go

in a strained relationship:

Back into it or away from it.

Either way, forgiveness

is the only key.

Chapter Thirty-Four

Hold Me Now, It's Hard For Me to Say I'm Sorry

A song by Peter Cetera of Chicago

When my mother died in September 2013, I thought the grief would gel the family into one. For siblings already separated from one another by distance, it would have been a cathartic moment to come together and share the burden of loss. Well, we did - but not for long. After the burial, we just disagreed on so many things that were so preposterously trivial it wasn't even worth anything that could change our life. It was the kind where small things gradually pile up over time to create such a humongous monster called animosity; a little mending here and there would have prevented it from becoming Frankenstein-size. But it is what it is.

As we wiped the dirt from our hands and walked away from the grave, we also walked away from each other - the farthest of all from our younger brother Joey.

Eight years later, we were still not talking to one another, albeit slowly for some, except for him, until one day, my sisters Suzette and Pinky decided

I should leave a message on the phone as he never answered our calls. The long and short of it is that we all flew to San Francisco on his birthday to see him. Arriving two days before his birthday, we finally holed up in a hotel room to fix everything that was broken. After all was said and done, we discovered that we had our own crosses to bear to even touch the other's, and many perceptions were wrong. If I were to sum up everything into one word that stood out after the dust had settled, it is Forgiveness.

Forgiveness is such a powerful word that changes the dynamics in people's relationships with one another. While there are only two directions you can go in a strained relationship: back into it or forever out of it, there's only one thing that can sway it either way: Forgiveness.

You can go two ways: forgive or don't. If it is difficult for you, then don't - go ahead, punish yourself.

Let the person you won't forgive - occupy your thoughts throughout your days and nights. They'd be like tenants in the upper loft of your mind and the luxurious chambers of your heart – occupying free of rent gratis et amore courtesy of your stubbornness. "What a life!" - these tenants would say. After all, you've invited them to stay there. For all their perceived mistakes, you are unkindly punishing yourself. Evict them for good. And the only good eviction would be a Notice of Forgiveness.

Dr. Tyler Vander Weele, co-director of the Initiative on Health, Religion, and Spirituality at the Harvard T.H. Chan School of Public Health, says, "Forgiving a person who has wronged you is never easy but dwelling on those events and reliving them over and over can fill your mind with negative thoughts and suppressed anger, yet, when you learn to forgive, you are no longer trapped by the past actions of others and can finally feel free." He says there are two types of forgiveness: Decisional and Emotional. Simply put, when we decide to do the act of forgiving another, it is called decisional. It is emotional when we forgive only within the bounds of our emotions. He says it is the emotional part that's difficult to do. Although we might do the decisional act of forgiving, deep inside, we haven't. And he says it does not happen at the flick of a finger. It takes a long time to do that and a lot of practice. Simple things like forgiving the guy who cut you in traffic or the guy who skips the line at a moviehouse queue – all these work towards your perfecting the act. But he says there's a scientific method to do this and calls it REACH.

1. *Recall.* Recall the occurrence that you were wronged and view it objectively. Revisit the situation as it happened and not think of the other person negatively nor let your self-pity stand in the way.

2. *Empathize.* Look at the occurrence from the other person's point of view. He could be going through something profoundly hurting, troubling or fearsome. They often don't think they've hurt others simply because they're already in a state of hurt, pain and fear.

3. *Altruistic Gift.* Altruism is the selfless and genuine concern for others without regard for your feelings - and that is a gift –

exhibited by no less than Christ Himself when He laid down His life for us. Think about that moment and apply it inversely this time. Have you ever been forgiven in your life? How did you feel?

4. *Commit.* You have to convince yourself to forgive and commit to it. Do not let it slip away from your thoughts. Commitment will move you to decide to forgive (decisional).

5. *Hold it.* When you've forgiven, hold it – forever. Don't take it back. No return, no refund – What you can do at Walmart or Costco, you can't do it here; otherwise, it'll cost you the healed relationship to break down again.

Inversely, while forgiving another is difficult, asking for forgiveness is. It takes a lot of courage to forgive another, but it takes even more to ask for forgiveness.

I am appalled at how people today try to downplay apologies subliminally and get around with even the simplest act of saying, "I'm sorry." I've seen someone on Instagram saying we can rephrase "I'm sorry" without sacrificing the giveaway of our ego. They say, instead of saying, "I'm sorry to bother you,"; say rather – "Is now a good time to ask you a question?" or instead of saying, "Sorry, I'll fix that," you say – "Thanks for pointing that out, is there anything else that I should know?" Although the good virtue of thankfulness takes over the apology, it'll hurt in the long run. Consider me old-fashioned, but "I'm sorry" is still the way to go.

Forgiveness should not just stay in your heart. Forgiveness, when not given away, is not forgiveness because you have retained it. That is why the spelling is ForGIVE - you have to *give* it away to put meaning into its honest and rightful context.

So, let me repeat it – forgiveness is such a powerful tool, but we seldom use it, and until we do that, we will never realize its full impact.

It is such an incredible power within us - and everyone has it. It is what we have in common, just like the air we breathe and the time we have on our hands.

I watched the movie Schindler's List not too long ago, and I've watched it at least four times. I love the scene where Oskar Schindler and the drunk Nazi camp commandant Amon Goethe are at the villa overlooking the camp one night. Goethe had been shooting prisoners at random from his balcony earlier that day.

The drunk Goethe falls on his chair and says to Schindler, "You're not drunk, and that is control. Control is power,"

Schindler sips his drink and says, "Is that why they fear us? They fear us because we have the power to kill arbitrarily. *Power is when we have every justification to kill and don't.*"

Goethe asks, "Is that power?"

Schindler answers, "That's what the emperor said. A man steals something, brought in before the emperor, and throws himself down on the floor as he begs for mercy. He knows he's going to die, and the emperor pardons him. This worthless man. He lets him go. That's power."

When we came together in that hotel room on the 19th day of November 2021, we all had that power within us – the power of forgiveness. And for all the eight years that that power was bottled up within us, we just watched each other fade away. But we also found the reason why we were all stuck – we had our own crosses to bear, and they had stood in the way. But we have also learned that through those years, our love for each other was just bursting at the seams, waiting to break free.

The love was all there but had nowhere to go because we kept it locked within our hearts. We all knew we had that power of forgiveness but did not use it.

Fr. Henry Alva, the Provincial of the Franciscan Capuchins of Mary, Mother of Good Shepherd Province of Canada, says it aptly, "couples generally do not fight because they hate each other or there is no more love. They fight because they still love each other. Otherwise, why bother?"

Again, the power to forgive, think about it.

That day, we felt what it is to have that power within us and what it can do, and how we saw it unfold to become even more powerful - when we gave it away.

Forgiveness is supposed to be free, but why do we keep it locked in our prison called *Fort Pride*?

The language of innocence

is

God's language

Chapter Thirty-Five

Vito: An Answer They Can't Refuse

My son recently moved with his family to Waterford, Ontario, some 111 kilometers from our house. As I was sorting out the things that they left so I could soon ship them out, one thing that caught my interest was a trilogy DVD of The Godfather, Parts 1, 2 and 3. I've always loved this movie, as my father did in his lifetime. He loved the movie so much that the rear vanity plate on his black 66 Mercedes 250S was "Godfather." I love the scene where Vito Corleone tells Johnny Fontaine in calm confidence that he is going to *"make an offer he can't refuse"* to the stubborn movie producer giving poor Johnny a hard time.

This movie reminded me of my grandson Vito, the baby Corleone in the house who made an offer that can't be refused.

Although born in Canada, Vito has always been spoken to in our Philippine dialect at home, and he fluently speaks it as a first language – even today. His parents feel that the native language is the only connection that will make him feel how it is to once belong to a great country. They said that inevitably, he'd speak English, learning it in school through his teachers and classmates anyway. Besides, they don't want his cousins back in the Philippines to feel left out when he goes back home to visit; and they want him and his sister Maia to interact well.

Down the road, he might lose it, but he can always say that once upon a time, he spoke it and spoke it well – rather than risk looking so pathetically puzzled like other children I've seen in this land when you talk to them in Filipino. I find it troubling to hear parents back home speak to their children in English like it was their first language. We are the only country in the world that forces our children to speak a foreign language right on the sacred soil washed by the blood of our ancestors defending the honor of our language. So, as a people, who are we? Let's just put it this way: Filipinos have constantly set their sights outward to the world, and that's a great thing. But that's another story.

When Vito first went to see the school principal for his Junior Kindergarten, she asked him, "Hi Vito, do you speak English?"

As his mom Yin was about to answer for him, the principal shushed her, motioning that Vito should reply.

Vito kept his head down, being the shy and silent boy he was (even today).

There being no answer, the principal asked him again, "Vito, do you speak English?"

Reluctantly, with his eyes still on the floor, he began – “Angel of God, my guardian dear, to whom His love...”

“Okay, okay...that’s good, Vito.”

Today he’s in Grade 5, and he’s trilingual. Filipino, English and the language of God.

Chapter Thirty-Six

Maia: A Refuse They Can't Answer

When Maia and Vito **were still small,** we'd spend summer weekends barbecuing in our backyard. There'd always be our best friends, Tito Bong and Tita Nenen (In Filipino, Tito means uncle, and Tita means auntie). We'd all talk about a thousand and one things or just one thing with a thousand and one words, and the kids couldn't have cared less. While we'd be lost in our gastronomic world of barbecue, Maia would be lost in her Barbie. Vito was the perpetual lonely planet spinning in his own galaxy.

On Tuesday morning, Nenen phoned Maria about a plant she wanted. Maria had the plant Nenen wanted for her condo. Maria told her to drop by the house anytime as somebody would answer the door for her.

Soon enough, there was a buzzer on the door. Maia rushed to the door to open it while I remained seated on the sofa, reading a book.

When she saw it was Bong, she said, "Why are you here, Tito Bong? *There's no barbecue today!*"

I had overheard the whole thing, and too embarrassed, I swiftly cut through the awkward wait for Bong's reply.

I said, "Bong, here's your plant."

All's well that ends well, I thought to myself.

The biggest room

in our hearts should

be the room of

Gratitude.

Chapter Thirty-Seven

Psalm 95 Your Day

As I write this, it is eight days before Thanksgiving Day. This chapter will be one of the long chapters in this book. It is about Gratitude.

The spirit of gratitude is supposed to occupy the biggest room in our hearts when we come to think that we don't deserve anything after that guy Adam ruined our immortality. We are now in the second phase of our lives after our redemption. So, it is but right that we give thanks.

In life, there is so much to be thankful for. I believe that if everyone is just grateful for everything and anything they behold in a day, it will be a better world to live in – no envy, hatred, jealousy, no covetousness but only peace, harmony, and contentment.

But in all honesty for myself, I don't know where to begin to give my thanks. As I contemplate my life, I stare out the window far into the distance for a long time, thinking through everything I've been blessed with – and I believe there's just a zillion. Every day I thank God for the gift of family, friends, and my life, but these are just as clichéd as can be.

As I think of what thankfulness should be, I feel that it should *not* be within the context of what I have and where I am in relation to the people and things that surround me, but instead on *who I am* and *what I can do* in relation to people and things that I surround myself with; and when I say this, it could also mean the greater passive world beyond where I sit. I must put this in the correct perspective in line with the values I dearly hold.

I acknowledge that I am just a delinquent tenant in this world who hasn't even paid rent but just the payback of stewardship of what has been entrusted to my care – the earth where I stand, the people that I love and care for, and the friends whom I walk with and lead.

And for all these tasks, I believe I am incapable of doing all these things alone by myself. I still need God's blessings to help me cope daily.

And for everything that I am thankful for, My self will be last in the order of things - not that I am ungrateful, but I am humbled by the fact that He has given me everything that I can ask for, even those that I do not deserve. I should come last, and others come first. My life is but a vessel made by the Lord to fill in with the things He wants me to share with others - Love, Understanding, Patience, Forgiveness, Faith, and the spirit of gratitude - and many more good things that could only come from Him.

And if I thank the Lord for every breath I take, saying a million thanks will never be enough.

At this exact moment, to be technical about it, I have breathed 534.9 million times, adding 22,000 to that at the end of this day. At a mathematical ratio of 1 to .0000000001872, I'd be the most ungrateful person in the whole universe to the power of a zillion if I have not even a bit of gratitude under my skin to give back.

There are just a few words heard over and over in our household on any given day. *God bless you; I'm sorry, I love you, take care, you're welcome, and thank you.* All these words help improve our world, and they need someone present to receive it. But it is the word *Thank You* that you can say *alone* as often as you can within the day and within the confines of your shell. You can whisper the word like a mantra every moment of your day. A feeling of wellness and happiness will engulf you when you do this.

Gratitude should not only be lived, felt, and said on Thanksgiving Day. Again, we should give thanks every chance we get at any minute and hour of the day.

As I rode with Leandro the other day to pick up Lorenzo from work, he waved his hand over the rear window as the driver slowed down to let him cut in. It was a small act of saying thank you, even if the other driver may not have seen it. And I thought to myself, that was good. At least Leandro felt good and was thankful for it.

Saying Thank You to another is a double-edged blessing. It makes the giver happy and the receiver even happier if acknowledged.

Being thankful reduces stress and improves our psychological, emotional, and mental state. Gratitude also reduces our propensity to compare ourselves with other people. Since we appreciate what we have, we do not look outward at what others have; we'd feel happier seeing them succeed. Like the purest water of life, being thankful dilutes all the toxicity that destroys our well-being.

Dr. Robert A. Emmons, Ph.D., a psychologist, and professor at the University of California Davis and a grantee of the Templeton Foundation researching young Christian teens dealing with the spiritual fruits of kindness, generosity, and selflessness, said in a study that being thankful is directly connected with a person's well-being. It increases happiness and subdues all negative feelings like depression and anxiety.

Every day, we should give thanks, even for the small things. For every gratitude that leaves our hearts, we gradually build a shield of invincibility, deflecting off all negative forces that attempt to pierce and destroy our day – anger, jealousy, resentment, and ill-will towards others.

This morning, as I drank my coffee and ate my croissant, I said, "Thank You, Lord, for this day. May you continue to use me for your great glory". After saying that, I still felt like not having said thank you at all – with all the things that I enjoy every day, there must be a way to say thank you and cover all these things.

As I write this, I can quickly think of a hundred blessings, but I will give you twenty. Going beyond this number might make you bored as it may no longer have relevance. But I would be grateful if you could look into your life and find that gem of gratitude inside you. When you see it, say thank you, God. It will open the floodgates of His storehouse of blessings reserved for you. Here's my twenty:

1. For waking me up today despite going to bed so tired late last night. One hundred seventy-eight thousand people will not open their eyes today, and there are 7,425 that will die at the end of this hour and every hour after that or 120 each minute. The Lord blesses me and keeps me still despite myself.

2. I am thankful that I woke up fine despite the still raging cases of COVID worldwide. There have been 618 million cases of people catching the virus, with 6.55 million deaths. As I write this, there were 355 thousand cases added today, according to the WHO. In my native country, there are 3.943 million recorded cases, with 62,882 deaths as of September 30. In Ontario, where I am, the total cases are 1.47 million, with 14.4 thousand deaths. Canada-wide, it is 4.28 million cases with 45,434 deaths. I am a lucky dude – truly blessed, to put it profoundly.

3. I am thankful that for all my stupid indiscretions, my wife Maria has firmly held the family within the bounds of the holy matrimony. The average divorce rate across all regions and all years is 4.08 per one thousand

marriages as of May 2022, according to an article by Psychologytoday.com – Divorce Rates Around the World Today: A Love Story. The lowest rate is in Sri Lanka, with just 0.45 percent, with the highest at 11.03 in Kazakhstan in Russia. Eastern Asia and the Pacific have relatively low rates. Surprisingly, one of the most notable predictors is the Gross National Product of a country, with the most developed ones having the highest rates. Those countries have more women in the workforce and higher education rates. Does it mean that the richer and more educated they become, the more likely they are to file for divorce? Indeed, something is missing. I take that it could be what Catholic countries have – they have a lower proportion. This study does not include the United States, which has not responded to the call to submit its figures. However, they've already been classified as an extreme outlier anyway – probably because it is still aggressively raging like a bull with its sharp horns against an institution formed together by God.

4. I am thankful that I have a good pair of shoes to walk around the neighborhood and do my daily hike, alternately using between two pairs depending on the distance I choose. Imagine your child going to school without shoes. If that won't make you cringe, I don't know what will - but there are 300 million people worldwide who cannot afford to buy even a single pair of shoes. Now there's a guy named Blake Mycoskie, the owner of Tom Shoes, who uses a business model called "One for One," i.e., he donates one pair of shoes for every one sold. When he visited Argentina

in 2006, he found out that many children could not even go to school for lack of shoes, and to his surprise, it was a microcosm of a bigger problem globally. A year later, he donated 10,000 pairs in Argentina. Every year they celebrate One Day Without Shoes Day to raise awareness of how it is to walk without shoes. Now, take a look at your closet. According to a study by Go Compare, the average woman owns 20 pairs but only regularly uses 5. You'll be surprised by the data on men in the current times. So, I also say thank you to people who care for others.

5. I am thankful to be in a place where the air I breathe is cleaner and fresher. The atmosphere is so polluted in other countries, making it hazardous even to live within the four corners of their homes. In a study of 529 major cities from 88 countries around the world, the top 5 are in south Asia, with Lahore, Pakistan, as the worst with 108 microns per cubic meter against the 5.0 annual limit set by the World Health Organization. Halifax, Canada, is within the Top 10 cleanest. Well, that's just within our neighborhood, so I am still so thankful.

6. I am thankful that I had a full breakfast meal this morning. Around the world, millions have not eaten their three full meals as of this moment. If I were to gauge how bad the problem is, I'd instead give you a picture of what hunger is in the wealthiest country in the world – the United States of America. From there, you go figure. According to National Geographic,

one-sixth of Americans don't know where to get their next meal. Their food stamps issued by the Supplemental Nutrition Assistance Program (SNAP) don't even stretch out to the next meal, and it's been pared down from US$206 a month to US$175. The US government has even subtly invented a new lexicon replacing "hunger" with "food insecure," probably to soften the image involving their country. But I want you to imagine other countries in the third world. What I fear will happen there is that people will snap. I am so blessed the coffee tasted good and the croissant was splendid.

7. With my grandchildren Maia and Vito, I am blessed to be among the 7.5 million grandparents in Canada. According to the General Social Survey of Statistics Canada, a government agency that just launched its Family Matters section - although the average age of grandparents has gone up from 65 in 1995 to 68 in 2017, they have fewer grandchildren (from 5 in 1995 to 4 in 2017) owing to women delaying their pregnancies. On the other side of the world, the Australian Bureau of Statistics (ABS), in its study in 2017, says that sometime between 2023 and 2029, the number of couples living without children will *overtake* the number of those living with them. Bronwyn Harman, an expert from Edith Cowan University's School of Psychology and Social Science, says it is a trend that will continue. So, if you're a grandparent now, you're blessed.

8. Finally, the role of women takes center stage. I am thankful for the latest development on the achievement and acceleration of gender equality for women and girls on the world stage when they recently launched at UNGA77 on September 13, 2022, the Sustainable Development Goal 5. It must have been interceded by the greatest woman of all time, the Virgin Mary.

9. I am thankful for a great coffee this beautiful morning. Although I had put in more coffee and sugar than my limits were, I felt warm and refreshed to kick off my day. For the lone croissant my boys have left for me on the table - they could have eaten it, but I believe they'd preferred to let me have it and instead get their breakfasts from some drive-thru. I feel blessed they still love me even if I'm difficult to live with.

10. I thank Leandro for watering the flowerpots on the front porch today. Typically, not him, but he did it. What's up, man?

11. For our Pomeranian Husky (Pomsky), who looked at me through Lorenzo's phone as they face-timed with the kids. He is a wonderful dog who has become part of us and knows his place in our hearts so well; he thinks he's the center of the universe. Well, for brief episodes in a day,

especially when he nuzzles me - but that's fine; he deserves it more than the occasional dog treats.

12. I am thankful for a great dinner last night with all my loved ones gathered around the table for Yin's birthday. The food was so good, but their presence trumped it all.

13. For Maia and Vito. I just got the most beautiful smiles from this duo today. Even with their braces, their smiles shone like a bright ray through the cloudy skies.

14. Profusely thankful for friends who never leave my side, no matter what.

15. Thankful too for difficult friends. Thank you for being my friend even though you make it difficult for me when all it takes is kindness. But then, I figured you need it more for the rainy days in your life, I understand. Perhaps you're my friend because I have so much unreleased forgiveness in my heart with nowhere to go.

16. I thank the Lord for Lorenzo, who darted out of his room last night to give me the priestly blessing, ending it with I Love you Dad I love you Mom, goodnight. His mom was already asleep in our room when he said it, so I shushed him, but he said it nevertheless.

17. I am thankful for Friday nights. Thank God it's Friday, four days from now! God must be wondering what's all this fuss about Fridays, but this is the day when all my kids glow up. Seeing them all excited and happy is enough reason to thank Him. Now, that's one of the fusses He can strike out from His list.

18. I thank the Lord for all the difficulties we have encountered in our life. We have learned to look hard into ourselves to find the strength to move on. For every beating we got, the scars made us stronger to face even more challenging battles. We would not be where we are today if God had walked far from us.

19. I thank the Lord for the food on the table, high-calorie or not. They nourish my body and soul; I feel blessed for this daily gift.

20. I thank the Lord for having known friends in the Brotherhood of Christian Businessmen and Professionals community. Through all the joys and sorrows, we have stood together, remained, and faced all odds. While many have fallen along the way, most have carried the banner forward. The battle for Christ is long-drawn and bitter, especially in an unfamiliar terrain where no one cares, and we must fully understand that. Each one is the wind beneath the wings of the other.

After you've looked into all your blessings and have said thanks, *Psalm 95 your day*. If you're wondering what I mean by this, read the following aloud.

Come, let us sing for joy to the Lord

let us shout to the Rock of our salvation.

Let us come before him giving him thanks

and extol him with music and song.

If you don't know the song, say it, and sigh a thank you.

He'll hear it.

Design your own

happiness.

CHAPTER THIRTY-EIGHT

OUR DESIRES IN LIFE

I CONSIDER THE DESIDERATA to be an embodiment of everything that makes life happy and fulfilled. Max Ehrmann of Indiana first wrote this poem in 1921 and registered it for copyright in 1927, even without a title. Whether or not this beautiful poem falls within the public domain today has remained hotly contested in many judicial fora, with the last suit only answered coldly by the US Supreme Court's silence and inaction. But it is such a beautiful work of prose that has perhaps inspired millions over the years. I lay no claim on it at all. I can only offer my thoughts along its lines and hope to provide paths we can all take to get to our own. Here goes:

Go placidly amid the noise and haste and remember what peace there may be in silence.

According to the World Health Organization, noise pollution is one of the most hazardous environmental threats to man's health. Records say that it had caused 16,600 premature deaths and more than 72,000 hospitalizations in Europe alone. Guangzhou in China is the noisiest, and Zurich, Switzerland, is the quietest. But amid all the noise and haste, we should not remain muffled in our communications and lose our voice. Let the voice within our hearts always rise above the din. Simon and Garfunkel's Sound of Silence says it all. We should not stop reaching out to one another. Soon, if it's not happening yet, people will stop talking to each other. The handwriting is on the wall today: in the subway trains, tenements halls, and dinner tables. *People are stuck to their phones*. People have become invisible. So, I say, reach out and let your voice be heard. Let the voice of peace be heard.

As far as possible, without surrender, be on good terms with all persons.

Hmm, easy to say. Hey, I know people who always insist to be correct and want to be known for it. For God's sake, they can be kind, but they'd rather be correct. And they're clueless why they're not on good terms with a lot of people. They have to stop thinking that everyone should bow down to their terms. Sometimes, those who withhold their opinions are the ones who's got the best solutions. They were just not given the chance to speak their minds. So, as you sit, look within your circle; look to your right, and look to your left. If you don't find them, it could be you.

Speak your truth quietly and clearly, and listen to others, even to the dull and the ignorant; they too, have their story.

I always knew that coming home to the place where I spent my youth would be a time well spent. There is something mystical in reliving something when you're actually in the same spot where things you've always imagined happened. Nothing beats seeing, hearing, feeling, and tasting the past in the same place with the same people. It's like being teleported back in time in HG Wells' Time Machine. I went home to the Philippines in 2017. On my first day, I left the hotel early morning and walked to the old neighborhood where I had spent my youth (my native city is so tiny you can practically walk anywhere and already be everywhere). There, I found my remaining friends. Over the same kind of beer, the same style of *kaldereta* (lamb stew), and the same sort of discordant music played on the guitar; I felt like time froze. They had the same old jokes - I could almost label them with numbers, so I didn't need to hear each one anymore. The conversations turned serious and nostalgic as the night wore on. As the music died, I listened to the same familiar stories of woe and regret – the usual should'ves. I should've done this; I should've done that. As I looked around, I only saw strange faces of weary old men battered by life. I had hoped to find the same exuberance of youth only to find the child within each one had long left past his bedtime.

But the stories were great. Although I've heard them a million times, I felt like I heard them for the first time. It seemed surreal, but it was real.

Avoid loud and aggressive persons; they are vexations to the spirit.

Proverbs 22:24-25 says, "Do not make friends with an angry man and do not go with a hot-tempered man, or you may learn in his ways and be tangled in spirit." People don't need to be loud to be aggressive. Some are silent and passive aggressors, and many look friendly, dignified, and innocent. Some are so full of drama you'd think for a moment they need empathy, only to find a dagger on your back as you turn to leave. Either way, they are a scourge to your spirit and an unwelcome intruder in your peaceful silence. Stay away in peace – you'll be better off without them.

If you compare yourself with others, you may become vain or bitter, for always there will be greater and lesser persons than yourself.

The only person you need to compare yourself with was the You yesterday. See if the You today is much kinder, better, and more forgiving and loving. If not, continue to work on it. Over time, you'll see the changes.

Enjoy your achievements as well as your plans.

My friend Ralph whom I've known since kindergarten said that there are three things a man should do in his life to be fulfilled:

Marry a good wife, plant a tree, and write a book.

I am so blessed the Lord has generously gifted me with all three.

Good Wife. Maria has stayed by my side for forty-two years. Through ups and downs, she has been gently steadfast in patience, forgiveness, and love - something I'm always in awe of and try to match but always end up short. After all my wayward ways, she has remained forgiving and loving to the family and me. I cannot find anyone like her, even if I have to vet the 3.905 billion women in the world. There is no place to see her in the home but the kitchen, where she loves to cook. She's so passionate about her cooking that nothing comes close to it except family and her love for God, which is supreme.

Plant a Tree. Back home, when the kids were small, I planted Gmelina trees. I've lined them up from our steel gate down the road up to my house on a hill and had strapped streetlamps around them so we'd feel safe when we get home at night. They are strong, deciduous, and sun-loving. The last time I checked, they've grown so high and massive that you can't wrap your arms around them. They were my boys' favorite place to become invisible in Hide and Seeks. Gmelinas are used to make great pulp and paper. This book in your hand right now could be a Gmelina. One day, when I get home, I'll plant some more so my great-grandchildren can run to and become invisible in Hide and Seeks. That way, I'll still know where they'll hide even when I'm too senile to guess.

Write a Book. So, the good wife kept on nagging me to write a book. This book is the product of that never-ending torment.

Keep interested in your own career, however humble; it is a real possession in the changing fortunes of time.

This line reminds me of two people: First is Joseph, the father of Jesus. Relegated to the background, he had mentored the boy Jesus in the humble trade of carpentry. He had never gone beyond this silent and unassuming role and yet had raised the world's greatest man and the Son of God. His role in Jesus' life was his real possession that has changed the fortunes of men for thousands of years.

The other person is John the Baptist. Unkempt, unshaven, dirty, and clad in rags, he was clear in his resolve and resolutely knew what his career was – to baptize all men, including the Son of God and pave the way for Him. One day, with all humility, he said, "He must increase, but I must decrease." I think this is the prayer we must all say every day.

In this book, I have talked about my career and how it possessed me. I am still raising the caveat here: God and family come first before your career. Once your career grips you in its claws, the fortunes of time might not be kind to you.

Exercise caution in your business affairs, for the world is full of trickery. But let this not blind you to what virtue there is; many persons strive for high ideals, and everywhere life is full of heroism.

Matthew 10:16 says, "I am sending you out like sheep among wolves. Therefore, be as shrewd as snakes and innocent as doves." People have taken shrewdness beyond its true Biblical meaning. Shrewdness must be within the context of what good we can obtain – never at the expense of another who suffers. Beyond the bounds of goodness and fairness, it becomes trickery. I still believe there is goodness in everyone, and many still stand on the high ground of great values. While we may not see this in everyone we meet, it doesn't mean it's not there. Good men are all around; they just remain silently humble.

Be yourself. Nuff said.

Especially do not feign affection. Neither be cynical about love; for in the face of all aridity and disenchantment, it is as perennial as the grass.

1 Corinthians 13:4-7. Love is patient. Love is kind. It does not envy; it does not boast. It is not proud. It does not dishonor others. It is not self-seeking, is not easily angered, and keeps no record of wrongs. Love does not delight

in evil but rejoices with the truth. It always protects, always trusts, always hopes, and always perseveres.

I could not say it any better.

Take kindly the counsel of the years, gracefully surrendering the things of youth.

In 2020, there were 6.8 million senior citizens in Canada out of a population of 37 million - roughly about 18%. The Philippines had about 7.0 million out of 110 million in the same year - a paltry 6%. Could this mean that older people in the Philippines are likely to die faster than in Canada? But this means that Canada has more older people and is comparatively an ageing population. Adding up, would this mean there'd be a bigger chance of wisdom being passed from the older generation to the young? Not at all. Wisdom comes from all ages. The world will be better if the old and the wise actively engage the youth in inter-generational conversation and vice-versa – and this should be for all in the world. But the world is so full of the 'Self' on both sides that wisdom can hardly thrive. Only if one is humble and genuinely listens can wisdom gently pass between generations. Socrates is right. True wisdom is knowing you know nothing.

Nurture strength of spirit to shield you in sudden misfortune. But do not distress yourself with dark imaginings. Many fears are born of fatigue and loneliness.

In life, for all your tribulations and misfortunes, fears, and anxieties - God can only offer you Psalm 46:10. And I think that's enough.

So, be still, and know he is God.

Beyond a wholesome discipline, be gentle with yourself. You are a child of the universe no less than the trees and the stars; you have a right to be here. And whether or not it is clear to you, no doubt the universe is unfolding as it should.

There are 200 billion trillion stars in the universe, and there are 3 trillion trees on earth. 7.75 billion people inhabit the planet Earth. Why the heck would you believe you have a right to be where you are right now? You are just a speck of dust less than 000000000.1 percent of earthlings traveling at the speed of light to nowhere, over an expanse of 92 billion light years away from an observable point of view of the universe.

So, my friend - you are not even a fraction of a trillionth of a speck in the whole universe. And how big is the universe for you? By converting into light-years (1pc=3.26ly), we get, with ze=1100 and H0=71km/s/Mpc, a value for the radius of the observable Universe equal to: R=1.343104Mpc=43.8Gly, or roughly 45 billion light years times 2.

Pretty easy, huh? (lol)

Well, forget about that gobbledygook and let's simplify this. Let's forget about the size and discuss your right to be here instead.

You have a right to be where you are simply because God created you in His exact image and likeness. He loves you so much that He created you to be his mini-me. And when you strayed away, He sent somebody He loved to bail you out. So, you're a spoiled brat who shouldn't even deserve a square inch of the universe if we think hard about it.

But here's the thing: God loves you, despite you.

And I think that's all that matters.

So, there's your declaration of rights.

Therefore, be at peace with God, whatever you conceive Him to be.

Who is he to you? What is he to you? What does he look like to you?

Authors Heinrich Weinel and Alban G. Widgery, in their book Jesus in the Nineteenth Century and After, said, *"To some, God and Jesus may appeal in a way other than to us: some may come to faith in God and to love, without a conscious attachment to Jesus. Both nature and good men besides Jesus may lead us to God. They who seek God with all their hearts must, however, someday on their way meet Jesus."*

So, whoever your God is, that's you, and we could be different. But let me tell you who's mine.

Don't be confused now, but he goes by many names to me. Alpha and Omega. The Light of the World. The Resurrection and the Life. The Good Shepherd. The Saviour. King of kings. Lord of lords. The Way. The Truth. The Life. The Prince of Peace.

I could go on and on and still point to the same guy. And He's the only one I got, and He's so good, I can't catch up in goodness. That's why I always make peace with Him every day. May I introduce Him to you?

And whatever your labors and aspirations, in the noisy confusion of life, keep peace in your soul. With all its sham, drudgery, and broken dreams, it is still a beautiful world.

We all look at the world by seeing it with our eyes, hearing its noise, laughter, and cries, and how people speak about it and live their lives in it.

But try this. Close your eyes and see it through the eyes of your heart. Feel it with your heart.

How you feel today - *that is your world.* Seize it now, as tomorrow it can change. But however it changes, it is still a beautiful world; maybe you did not see it that way the first time. So, look again.

Be cheerful.

This book is full of stories about how to be happy. What makes people happy, and how you make others happy. So, live the life you want and be happy no matter what. Be crazy and be cool with it. Laugh all you want, loudest if you may and infect the whole world. Then love unconditionally and expect little back.

So, Live, Laugh and Love. Mix these three in a tall glass, and throw in prayer and a dash of faith. Then, at the top of your lungs, shout to the world: Cheers!

Strive to be happy.

Only you can define it; no one else can.

As you reach the summit,

be ready to discover that

it may just be the bottom

of yet another mountain.

CHAPTER THIRTY-NINE

THE NET WORTH OF LIFE

YOU'RE RICHER THAN YOU THINK

IT IS ALMOST HALLOWEEN as I write this. Welcome to the ghoulish world of giant tarantulas, horrifying clowns, pug-nosed witches, ravenous cannibals, deranged mental patients and zombies – all to haunt you. But Halloween or not, there's something that could haunt you forever -

It's the mistakes that you made in your life.

Over the weekend, I had friends I've known since kindergarten visit me from New York. I had a Leonardo and three Manuels: Manuelito, Emmanuel and Manuel. Joining us was a local classmate without Tom and Dick – Harry Black. They drove north for ten hours to Toronto, three hours of which were probably spent in roadside-stop restrooms to ease their prostate woes. The conversations could have been bland, but thanks to Belgian mademoiselle Stella Artois and a Scottish gentleman named Glenfiddich who added their bit to the fun.

We avoided one topic though: the mistakes of the past.

Somehow, doing that would expose the vulnerabilities of each, and that wouldn't be too kind and gentle to one who's probably had enough missteps in their life. At our age, we've seen and done all.

While at some point, people acknowledge the mistakes they've made in their life, it's the lessons they've learned that they'd rather talk about - and that's what we did.

What I've seen was very different from what I've held over the years. Across the table were the crinkly faces gradually ravaged by the ebb and rush of time; too conspicuous were the crow's feet under their eyes, now beclouded by cataracts around the pupils; easily noticeable too were the gnarled and knotty fingers that held the curvaceous waist of Stella. But the happy mediocrity of student days never seemed to have left them every time the raucous laughter between sips would erupt. Clearly, through the weary souls and the aching bones, the desire to live out life to the max still shines bright like the Luxor Lamp of Las Vegas. As everyone agreed, the great conversations were to stay in Vegas.

Everyone around the table was retired. It was easy to think that each may have come to contend with existential relevance and usefulness at some point.

So, let me draw a lesson from all that.

Life is like a pencil.

Pencils, in a case, don't mean anything – until you use them. But to be useful, you need to do four things:

First, like a pencil, sharpen yourself from time to time.

My good friend, retired convent nun Sister Tomasita, told me a story about an old man who could neither talk nor walk. He'd sit in his wheelchair all day long, and it seemed his usefulness had long left him chasing a thrill. But in family gatherings where he'd sit, his mere presence keeps everyone reined in – out of respect and deference. *That was his usefulness.*

But we are not in a wheelchair. Beyond our presence, there are many things we can do. All it takes is some imagination that will always keep us sharp.

Pencils lose their sharpness as we keep on using them to write. As people get old, their usefulness also seems to dull away. So, how do we sharpen ourselves?

Find a hobby and share it.

Do gardening. Share your garden veggies with a neighbor.

Plant flowers. Give your wife a flower every day.

Find something worthwhile to do and help someone. Fix a child's bike.

Upgrade whatever skills you got and teach somebody. Paint, draw, and write a poem.

Bake bread. Break bread with a long-lost friend.

For a pencil, imagine the pain of being whittled down by a sharp knife, but the pain of being sharpened keeps it useful.

It is the same with people.

The greatest sharpeners are the pains and struggle one must go through in life. There is a natural process of whittling out all the rough edges and dullness that one gradually undergoes over time. It takes fortitude of character, grit, resilience, and the great values of forgiveness to finally emerge sharp again.

People evolve to become stronger when they suffer. In the end, betrayal, heartbreaks, rejection, cheating – all the whittling makes them sharp and valuable.

The second thing to do is *correct all our mistakes* along the way.

That is why a pencil has an eraser. Like a pencil, we can erase the mistakes we make from time to time. But to do that, it is crucial that we first acknowledge those mistakes - then erase them, but always remember to keep the lessons. On a clean slate, catch up with the opportunity to re-write a new chapter in your life story and make it beautiful. It is never too late to do that. Although there is no guarantee that you can perfect it, it is always worth a try.

The third thing to do is - like a pencil, *leave your mark.*

Do something good for someone beyond your usual for friends, family, and even strangers. Buy an extra breakfast meal for someone out in the street; hold the door for some old folk behind you. Donate anonymously to a charity. Make a difference in someone's life. I once did volunteer work for a Toronto charitable company sorting out used toys for Christmas, and I found it so fulfilling it brought me back in time to when I was a small boy - feeling like the whole warehouse of toys was all mine. Make the hollows of your footprints gather inspiration so people who follow your path won't get lost. Like the bread crumbs Hansel and Gretel left on their tracks to guide their father, let the kindness you do for others guide those who search what its definition is.

The fourth thing to do is *look into your value.*

Just like a pencil, what is inside the wood is its soul. What the lead is to a pencil, the soul is to you. Since it is unseen, it is frequently undervalued and mostly unappreciated. Build fortitude, but fill it with happy things – love, compassion, forgiveness. Never sell it to the devil; he can't afford your value anyway – unless you undersell yourself.

Since I'm coming from a banker's point of view, I say that your soul is your net worth. Keep it where it is loved and appreciated for its value.

Bulked bottled water costs about $0.15 each at Walmart, $0.21 at Costco, $1.99 at some fancy restaurant, and $5.00 at the airport or on a flight. Look, it's the same commodity but priced differently according to location! So, just like bottled water, go where you are valued.

Avoid the places where your worth is not seen and appreciated. Beyond areas, carefully choose the people you surround yourself with. Keep your distance from people who put you down and don't see your worth, but always take the lessons you learn from it to heart. Sometimes, not knowing where you stand in someone's life is the exact spot where you stand because if someone truly values you, they wouldn't leave you guessing where you stand in their life. You must go where your positive energy is valued, celebrated, and returned.

Everyone you meet in life should see a value in you, or you see a value in them. There is always a lesson we learn from any engagement. Everyone you meet serves a purpose in your life. Make no mistake about it.

That is why I always say you never meet the wrong person in your life. And I've said this to friends who refuse to engage in conversations with people not on their level. Good or bad person, smart person or idiotic person, they all teach you a lesson. You could be the wrong person in their life, but you could also be a blessing when they've learned something from you and vice versa.

Let us remember that God does not give us the people we want. He gives us the people we need for us to grow. While it is true that people can hurt us along the way, we should come out sharpened because of that engagement. Never mind the hurt. Just remember the lesson, as they say.

But hurt or not, the challenge is to keep moving toward the direction *where we can be useful, where we can leave a mark, where we can correct past mistakes, and where we can lead,* and we can never do that without moving forward.

So, always keep a good attitude to get altitude. As we take small steps one at a time with our pockets full of lessons learned, we become better than we were yesterday. Remember that you reach higher than before for each step you struggle with. Always keep the attitude of resilience and perseverance until you succeed.

Do not stop walking and climbing until you reach the summit of whatever you aspire for – but always be ready to discover that it may just be the bottom of yet another mountain - because that's life.

After a hearty breakfast that Monday morning, I walked my friends to their car.

Still, beyond the creased foreheads, the crow's feet eye corners, and the knotty fingers were the smiles of naughty kindergarten kids – all too familiar yet strange.

As I gave them a bear hug each, I whispered –

"Keep moving. Keep walking."

Chapter Forty

The End

This is no B.S., but in the summer of '70, after Xavier's last day of school, I went straight to a records store called B.S. Electrical in our city.

There were the irresistible LPs of Paul Anka's 21 Greatest Hits. Also displayed was the every-groovy-kid-must-have-album of The Bee Gees - To Love Somebody. Then there was the every-parent-must-have Ray Conniff's Jean album which featured the Motown hit Aquarius, Let the Sunshine In.

Why would I choose any of those over the 1969 Beatles' Abbey Road album? After the Yellow Submarine LP, fans were ripping their hair out for the next, which was this. Unbeknownst to me, though, was that this would be The Beatles' last album together before they walked to Splits Ville across the zebra crossing.

When Maria and I went to the U.K. in the summer of 2019, it was the Abbey Road album's 50th anniversary. I packed my faded denim, light blue workman's clothes, and soft brown mid-cut brushed-suede shoes with crepe soles – precisely like the one worn by George. I had thought of doing an uncanny parody of the crosswalk of George Harrison while Maria does John Lennon. We chose these two for their contribution to improving this world with their music. For a time, the world sang in harmony with their songs, which is a good thing. These two who have gone ahead to a different celestial Apple studio must now be turning in their graves protesting why a baldie did a sneaky remake without a toupee and a woman doing the John Lennon.

The Abbey Road album is one of the most easily recognizable music albums ever. According to The Rolling Stones magazine, The Beatles' Sgt Pepper's Lonely Hearts Club Band album is the number 1 most recognizable album of all time, and at 4th spot is Abbey Road. Photographer Lain Macmillan only took six shots of the band using his Hasselblad camera while standing on a stepladder as a policeman halted the traffic – and you got this album.

When we were in London, I asked Paolo's girlfriend Philline to take us to Abbey Road. She knew her directions well, as we got there in no time. We finally saw the zebra crossing at the southernmost end of Abbey at the junction of Grove End Road in the St. John's Wood Area of northwest London.

We saw about a hundred fans, mainly north of fifty, all giggly and excited as they waited for their turn to do their crosswalk. As each group took their turn doing the walk, polite London cabbies and lorry drivers would kindly oblige, bemused, and stop for all the shapes and sizes wanting to look like the Beatles. Maria and I did about ten takes - quite a shame for the Beatle's six.

All told, I would like to make this point: I am choosing the Beatles' Abbey Road album to end this book for five reasons.

1. The Abbey Road album was their last recording as a group; as such, it was their final album. I am taking the contrary position on this one. I will not say this is going to be my last book. I'd say this will hopefully be my first of many a-coming. This chapter is the closing part of this book, so I feel that this album represents a significant and cool closing — a groovy thing - as they'd say in the '70s.

2. The Abbey Road crosswalk by The Beatles is perhaps the shortest road walk (Neil Armstrong's "one small step for man" was a moonwalk) that has captured the attention of modern historians. It is just approximately 26 feet in width, yet the significance of crossing it has captivated many generations, judged by the number of fans – young and old who patiently wait for their turn to do the walk. The Beatles actually "walked away" from the studio's direction in the picture. The symbolism here would be that after you read this book, you will *"walk away" from your Old Self towards your New Self.* What was 26 feet walk for The Beatles would be just this short read for you. I hope this book has

provided you with the road map as you walk the zebra crossing within yourself.

3. The attire chosen by The Beatles was a symbol of the demise of their group. After this album, they disbanded, with John quitting first (that's why he was the first in the line doing the walk). Reviews had it that this Abbey Road photo session was to be a funeral of the band based on what they wore. George was the gravedigger, Paul was the corpse, Ringo was the congregation, and John was the priest. *After reading this book, it will be a funeral of all the negative things in your life* that have stood in your way while you searched for yourself. Let all the negative things in your life die and fall facedown into the grave but let all the good vibes live within you as you walk across to the other side of the Zebra lines within yourself. Always remember that happy things live forever.

4. I love the songs in this album. As I wake up in the mornings, there's always a song in my head and not a few times had me humming George's Something and Here Comes the Sun, which are great songs, and it is for the love of their music that inspired me to pick the way this book shall end.

5. This Abbey Road album has a song entitled "The End" for its last cut.

So, to end this book - let me quote the lyrics of that song:

Oh yeah, all right

Are you going to be in my dreams tonight?

And in the end

The love you take

is equal to the love you make.

And that, my dear friends, is $\mathbf{E=mc^2}$**.**

EPILOGUE

SO, THAT'S IT.

I have just crossed the boundary of my dreams and whatever imagined limitations that kept me from going beyond its realms. When I was a young boy, my mom called me Don Quixote every time she saw me with my head above the clouds. But truth to tell, I always was (as probably all boys my age did), although I believe it was more her way of kicking my butt off from lazing around. I still chase windmills to this day. It's hit-and-miss, but this book is a hit as it comes to fruition.

We all need to spin away to where our dreams find fulfillment. With all the challenges and perceived boundaries that confront us every day, we are wont to Walter-Mitty our life unless something jolts us into action. I now dare you to find the spark that will change your life's trajectory, then gather the courage and grace to move further and higher. Do your part of the equation to make things happen, as God is constantly doing His.

I challenge you to pierce the myth that says you can't do the things you've always wanted to do. Damn the age! Remove the "can't" from your daily utility of words for the things that you dream of. *Do not go gentle into that good night. Rage! Rage against the dying of the light!* (Dylan Thomas)

I am thankful that some friends asked me for more stories beyond my social media postings. They have shoved me beyond my imagined boundaries. The tricky part was how to craft my prose in the way that I now live my life because old habits have nine lives.

To the dismay of our Jesuit superiors, when we did the high school Yearbook, the language used was consistent with how we behaved in class – irreverent, direct-to-your-face, devil-may-care demeanors - profane and cheeky. But we were damnably true to our feelings. It was our high school moderator Edison M who taught us how to go beyond our conventional enclosures to find our true voice – and when we did, he could have wished he'd withheld it (lol) – we were acerbic in oral and written prose, but we'd become the real us. On its last page, in bold letters, we screamed, *"we could have used decent words, but we don't want to sound phony."* The same holds for this book, minus the cusses and profanity, and I admit that it could have been cheeky at times. Throughout, I was careful not to sound like Holden Caulfield, now feeling too old to fill into his sneakers, and yet I thought that the message would be more faithful to its substance if I said it in the way that I did. There was still the angst and the irreverence, but I had to be true.

For the love of God, I believe I can still wear His armor, defend, and fight for the glory of His name, even with such a style of prose. When we're out on a battlefield as big as life – all too secular and unforgiving, we have to be armed in a language it understands to let it know that we can play its game. God's warriors have been using Sun Tzu's art of war long before the guy first saw the light of day in China.

All of us come into this life naked and with nothing. Solely on this basis, we are all gainers, and even if we sometimes think we lose, we actually gain. We gain experience. We gain lessons. We gain resilience. We gain friends and family. We gain their love, even if we may have lost it in the end, but still, we shall have gained, if only for the experience and lessons learned. There is only one thing we lose, and nothing else – Time. But that's it.

I hope this book will take you where you will find your true self. You are pre-destined to become the person you must be, and I think it would be a tragedy for you to get lost trying to find it. Let all the lessons you learn direct your steps to the right place where you find yourself. And since you take nothing out with you, share your lessons with others. Ultimately, we will all become better versions of ourselves when we leave and share these so others may learn.

Fyodor Dostoevsky had already written about my life story long before I was born. I saw myself playing in his book The Idiot. When I first faced this world, I came with all good intentions, integrity, and honesty, only to have my innocence tarnished and fall prey to its ways. Prince Myshkin entered the morally bankrupt Russian society like an innocent child-like Christ in his interaction with everyone. They mistook his goodness - calling it a weakness and idiocy and taking advantage of it. Not a few times was my silence mistaken for idiocy and weakness, and people took advantage of it. I am far from being Christ-like, and up to this moment, I still strive to at least live up to two of His greatest commandments. I know I can never perfect it and could even die trying, but at least nobody can say I did not attempt. I pray the same for you as you read this.

In the end, either you influence the world, or it sucks you in - which way will depend on the road you take. All you need to do now is take one step at a time – and each step that you take should bring you closer to who you are.

Stay the course.

Do not get lost.

ACKNOWLEDGMENTS

The seed of this book was a challenge sown at me by my son Adolfo Benjamin "Popoy," who said I should create a blog. Gwendolyn R Garcia had egged me long ago to put my thoughts in writing, but nothing came out of it. After sitting in the dark abyss of procrastination for what seemed like an eternity, my wife Maria picked up on it. My former workmate Bernadette P. Astudillo threw the same challenge, calling it now a book. So, here it is. I would like to thank you all for believing in me.

To my beautiful niece Samantha Cuerquis, thank you for initially editing this book and throwing in great creative writing suggestions. Also, her mom, my sister Pinky, thank you for reading this and following up with Sam on the editing. One day, I hope you both can translate this into French so I'd chance on some mademoiselle reading this at Cafè de Flore along the Boulevard St Germain. Big thanks to Allistair McDougall for the corrections, Simone Beaufort for the final editing, and Diane Miller for the final proofreading – you're all just awesome, I can't ask for more.

To Bob and Pauline Lloren for giving me a good book when we first met. That book may have taught me how to express myself in a way that could subvert William Strunk & EB White, but I'm doing this book my way because I don't think I could TED this. I can live with it as long as I deliver the message, but I dare you to finish this book in eighteen minutes. For that, I will always consider you my mentors, even beyond this regard, to include the soul's affairs.

Thank you to Etchin and Marilyn Sumagang for the wisdom and understanding of where the Lord wants us to be in our service to Him. Your life story parallels my own family's struggle against the ways of the world. For all that, keep inspiring others.

To Rey de Guzman, Ed Cunanan, Alex Mangahas, Marc Cavada, and Romy Pingol for sometimes being clueless about where I was, especially when I answered your texts long after the battles were over – I was writing this book. I appreciate your patience – but I know you have an infinite stash of it.

A big thanks to Rey S. Tan for allowing me to name my Grade 1 teacher in this book, Mrs. Providencia S. Tan – probably the greatest teacher in the world – like everyone's mothers.

I know this is long overdue, but thanks to Knicky Peralta for the use of your house. It was an excellent HQ for the lost, the tired, and the bombed-out. But I would still not touch your guitar. One of the reasons is that it's always out of tune aside from the long wait for my turn while others take too long learning their chords on it.

Thanks to Al Sun for contacting your brother Nilo Chito Sun. Getting a Yes answer from him to be named in the book as the flat-top kid was a long shot, but it gave me a great feeling. I always knew Chito's English would boom worldwide, not only within the halls of the World Bank.

Big thanks to the other kid, Fr. Art Borja, S.J. Your devotion to our Blessed Mother Mary is now in action beyond your elocution. Keep on infecting the world with your great sense of humor. In this regard, you're really still a kid.

Lei Bernabe, keep that sweet smile - I always knew you were sweeter deep within, aside from the great wisdom there.

A big thanks and hugs to Gigi Gurl del Rosario for allowing me to talk about Chuck. His story should be an example to those who get confused when faced with so many options in life regarding our faith. Chuck only chose one.

Brother Jay So, go out and travel the world and have fun but remember you can't take a beer across airport security checks. Keep the "you" that Agnes loved.

Thank you, Aurora "Nene" Bajarla, for the friendship. You don't know how to sing, so play Norwegian Wood on your Spotify AirPods instead.

You don't want Jonathan to sing it to you tonight while alone in your room.

Thanks to Jun and Annabelle Torres for distracting me while I was about to craft my speech. Such a sweet distraction worked to my advantage. Also, to Robert and Mai (Sabanal) Torres for inviting me to Robert's 60th. Keep up the good work. Never stop creating an infinite ripple.

Thanks also to Carlos "Litoy" Cecilio for saying Yes to Ralph's inclusion here. He was such a great influence on me in world history. He should pat you on the back for saying yes to me – I'm telling you this in advance so you'll not freak out when he does.

To Philip and Ellen Abalos, thank you for inspiring us to do charity work. You keep on doing it. The kids at Boystown are always eager to see you again.

Thanks, too, for the great wisdom, Fr. Henry Alva, the provincial of the Franciscan Capuchins of Mary, Mother of the Good Shepherd. You're the best marriage counselor on the planet.

I also have to thank Good Shepherd Sister Tomasita Antigua – you've added to my learnings about life with the wisdom of the readings you shared with me.

To my professor Edison Morales, my everlasting gratitude. Your students would have stood up at their desks and exclaimed, "O Captain, my Captain," if you got into trouble for teaching them how to break away from the conventions of youth – but we still think wearing pastel orange trousers with a tucked Barong Tagalog is an idea whose time has not come.

Thanks to our close friends: Bong and Nenen San Agustin. We have new plants for you. Our family doctor won't let us eat barbecue anymore, so let's just enjoy our drives next autumn in a four-seater Mustang convertible.

I say thank you to Allen Bacarro for constantly checking up on me. Don't play tennis anymore; balls should be smaller as we age. Start playing golf because the era of marbles is not too far off. Boys begin with marbles and end as old men playing marbles. Let's slow down, as tennis is a speed game. But hey, thanks so much for being a good friend. Thank you to Manuelito Enerio, Emmanuel Adecer, Manuel Fortich, and Leonardo Requerme for visiting me from New York. For long drives, drink less water next time (lol). Your visit has meant so much to me. Now, I know where conversations would lead after just one bottle of beer – the sofa bed.

To my kindergarten classmate Ralph Paguio, thank you for setting up the gold standard for legacies by adding book writing. As you see, I never forgot the conversation about this. This book completes that.

Thank you for the patience and kindness of heart of my sister Maria Socorro "Suzette" and her husband Ricardo "Dicky" Jacutin, as well as my brother Adolfo Ramon "Joey" and wife Josefina "Jing" Balinado. You have shown the world what forgiveness means.

To Popoy, Yin Maia, Vito, Blu, Paolo, Philline, Lorenzo, Leandro, and Maria L, I love you with all my heart. I couldn't say it any better than that.

And thank you, dear reader, for your time reading this. It's been nice talking to you. Finally, there's you. I'm tired of talking to myself for a long time. I hope you have picked a line or two you can keep while you walk the road within yourself. We're all together in this life whether you like it or not.

God bless you always.

Manufactured by Amazon.ca
Bolton, ON

31867824R00169